A Dream Worth Living

Finding Strength in the Depths of Struggle
Along the Continental Divide

Andy Amick

Pale Spruce, LLC
books@palespruce.com
www.palespruce.com

Editing by Kristi Amick
Cover Design by Chris Dobbs
Cover Photo by Nic Handy
Interior Photos by Andy Amick unless otherwise noted
Book Layout ©2017 BookDesignTemplates.com

A Dream Worth Living / Andy Amick. -- 1st ed.
ISBN 978-1-5390-9361-9

This is a work of narrative nonfiction. Dialogue and events herein have been recounted to the best of the author's memory.

To my wife Kristi -
Without your support and unending love,
my dreams would never become reality.

Acknowledgements

Without my family's support, I'd still be just a guy dreaming about adventures. Tyler and Logan, I hope you chase your dreams like you let your dad chase his. Kristi, your love imprinted itself on every mile of my race and every word of this book.

To my wonderful parents, who I still admire and look up to, none of this would be possible without you. Mom, thanks for not breaking all of my crayons and for putting up with my stubbornness. Dad, thank you for teaching me the value of hard work and honesty.

To my in-laws, Steve and Jeanne, thank you for always supporting my bike endeavors, even when you thought they were crazy. Steve, we miss you and your soothing presence.

Thank you to my brother, Erik, who taught me the finer points of riding two wheels through technical terrain. I know I can always count on you.

To Stan Williamson, thank you for getting me started on the wonderful adventure of mountain biking. Your guidance has been invaluable in my cycling and my career.

A huge thanks to Brion Antinoro for pushing me into the Tour Divide. You are a true friend. Your inspiring words during the race kept my pedals turning.

To Nic Handy, the finest bike handler and mechanic I've ever met. You do it all with such a calm, patient manner, and your craftsmanship is unparalleled. Thank you for letting me share the last days of the race with a friend like you.

Joe Tonsager, another amazing craftsman. Your attention to detail produced bikepacking bags that held up through the toughest of conditions. Thank you for your friendship and support during the race.

Alpha Bicycle Company, thank you for creating one helluva bike shop and your continued focus on quality.

To my friends at St. Luke's United Methodist Church (including the Lee, Lauer, Antinoro, Slade, Mostowy, Alderson, Van Hoosen, Levine, Sharpe, Barnard, Canaday, and Hollyman families), you are a true example of a community of grace. Thank you for such a warm welcome when I returned home, and your continued support during the writing process.

To my fellow 2014 Tour Dividers, you're as tough as nails. Dan, Casey, Alice, Sarah, and Ken - I treasure the days we rode together, pushing further than we thought possible.

For everyone that followed along with the race, your support did not go unnoticed. I appreciate all of the well wishes and kind words.

Chris Dobbs, thank you for the cover design and answering all of my pesky questions.

A special thanks goes to Kent Peterson and Jill Homer for their intriguing stories that led me to dream about racing the Tour Divide.

And finally, to my wife (and unpaid editor) again. I don't understand how one person has enough patience to put up with my riding and my writing. Thank you for sharing your life with me.

Contents

PART ONE

Survive

Press forward. Do not stop, do not linger in your journey, but strive for the mark set before you.

— GEORGE WHITEFIELD

1

Racing the Storm

MAJESTIC MOUNTAINS ROSE UP TO my right. A valley, green with tall grass, spread to my left until it gave way to more mountains in the distance. A lonely ribbon of dirt road rolled out in front of me. Behind me and to the west, the dark clouds of a thunderstorm threatened to engulf me.

Come on, pedal faster. Come on, don't let it catch you.

The ninth day of my 2014 Tour Divide race found me climbing alone in Montana, tantalizingly close to the Idaho border. At the border, the route turned downhill, and I knew I could outrun the storm. But could I reach the border before the storm caught me?

Come on, pedal faster. Come on, it's only a few more miles.

This section of road followed a zig-zag pattern. Each time the road zigged north, the storm reached out and tried to pull me into its cold darkness. I fought back, pedaling harder to reach the next zag in the road. Turning east with a tailwind, I would pull away from the storm's reach and the onslaught of rain.

Come on, pedal faster. Come on, you can beat this storm.

The zigs and zags continued. On that last day in Montana, this rider was going to win. I would not be caught by the storm.

Come on, pedal faster. Come on, pedal faster.

The Tour Divide is a 2745 mile mountain bike race from Banff, Canada to the US-Mexico border at Antelope Wells, New Mexico. The route climbs over 200,000 feet as it roughly parallels the Continental Divide through a combination of forest service roads, farm roads, trails, and pavement.

As an "underground" race, there are no entry fees or awards for top finishers. Instead, there are two simple rules. First, riders must be self-supported by carrying their own gear, food, and water. The only required item is a SPOT tracker, a small GPS device that records a rider's location and allows people to follow the race progress online. Second, non-commercial outside assistance is prohibited. This includes meeting friends or family along the route, pre-arranged lodging, and even accepting a bottle of water from a stranger. You must utilize establishments and businesses available to all racers.

There are no checkpoints, no support vehicles, no rest stops full of Gatorade, bananas, and energy bars. Each rider must make their own way down the spine of the Rocky Mountains with the goal of getting to the border as fast as possible. Some choose to ride deep into the night, stopping to pitch a tent by the side of the road and sleep for a few hours before pushing onwards. Others schedule their days around a full night's sleep in a hotel room to prepare them for what may lie ahead the next day. Most riders choose a combination of camping and hotel stays.

The opening 300 miles challenges riders with isolated Canadian wilderness. Once in Montana, racers pass through at least one town or outpost each day, often encountering fellow participants in the restaurants, hotels, and occasional bike shop. When leaving town, concerns revolve around wildlife encounters and snow covered passes instead of food and water supplies.

As the route approaches Mexico, the distance between towns increases; riders become more isolated, and food re-supply becomes an important factor. It is not uncommon for a racer to carry five liters of water and two days of food in New Mexico, adding more weight to a bike that is already loaded down with gear.

Throughout Canada and Montana, almost every mile had been a struggle in horrible riding conditions. I battled rain, snow, mud, freezing temperatures, numbness in my hands, and two extremely sore Achilles tendons. Taking advantage of a flatter day of riding and cruising my way into Idaho (even if I got soaked in the process) would have been a smarter choice to ensure my aching body would hold up for the remaining miles.

However, this was my day when the race became something I could thrive in, not just suffer and survive. Instead of taking my lumps and accepting that the storm would catch me, I pushed harder and harder on the pedals. I still had over 1700 miles to go in the race; pushing this hard wasted valuable energy that could come in handy later on.

Forget later.

I wanted to race and beat the storm that had been chasing me for three hours.

I was going to beat this storm. I was going to make it not just to Idaho, but Wyoming, Colorado, and then through New Mexico to the finish.

Come on, pedal faster. Come on, pedal faster.

I had dreamed of this ride for more than five years. I spent the previous year getting "ready" for the race - long training rides, testing gear, figuring out which food options worked best while riding all day, and going on overnight bikepacking trips to test out my complete setup. Once the race started, it took another week of suffering through horrendous weather before it felt like I was actually racing the Tour Divide.

My twenty years of mountain biking - from the mud and roots in South Carolina to the long climbs of Colorado - and my year of Tour Divide preparation were finally aligning in the form of enjoying the race and feeling alive.

2

My Bike Story

MY STORY STARTS BACK IN the 1980s. Growing up in South Carolina, bike riding was something we did around the neighborhood. Racing bikes was not something any of us kids dreamed about. We dreamed about football, monster trucks, and motorcycles. My football dreams were dashed very quickly - weighing in at under 100 pounds going into high school does not bode well for becoming an NFL middle linebacker. Little did I know that decades later being the smallest kid on my football team would turn out to be beneficial and ideal for cycling.

I remember my first "real" mountain bike, a red Schwinn from a local bike shop. Trails wound through the trees in our two-acre yard and became my training grounds. I was hooked on trying to ride the tightest trails. My technical riding days began with loop after loop around my house.

Like most kids, my bike riding stalled a bit when I started driving. My red '62 Fairlane was much more fun than my red Schwinn.

During my freshman year of college, I worked at a company putting together computers piece by piece. (Kids, yes there were times when we had to build computers from scratch, and they didn't come with a touch screen, an app store, or even the internet.) My manager, Stan Williamson, was also a cyclist and the fun technical trails of Harbison State Park called to us, just a mile from our office. We agreed to ride twice a week after work during the summer.

When quitting time finally arrived, we changed into our bike clothes, hopped on our bikes, and rode out to Harbison. We started with one lap and worked our way up to three laps of the main trail by the end of that summer.

We developed a tradition of racing back to the office after our laps at Harbison. There was no strategy or drafting or setting up for the final few meters. This was a drag race that began as soon as bike tires entered the business complex and didn't end until one of us made it back to the office. Some days Stan won by huge margin. Other days I won. Regardless of the winner, our rides always ended with both of us smiling and completely out of breath.

All of the training brought me to my first bike race: the Cactus Cup in Atlanta, Georgia. Other than a tree that jumped out at me during a test lap (more on that later), the race was a success.

At my local shop, the owner Steve and mechanic Layne took me under their wings, putting up with me hanging out in the shop at lunch and after work. During one of those days, I met newlyweds Mark and Denise, who were both into mountain biking. We became instant friends as we rode the local trails, ventured to a few races in North Carolina, and enjoyed a lot of time centered around bike riding. We rode through plenty of tight, muddy singletrack, all while making jokes about one another and enjoying the freedom the bike allows.

Even with the bike riding and racing in the southeast, I had a desire to move out west to explore the great big mountains of Colorado and Utah. Part of this was driven by the vacation my family took to Utah during my senior year of high school. The rest was driven by my ex-girlfriend who dumped me when she discovered that the party lifestyle of college was more fun than me, the crazy computer-nerd bike rider. When put in those terms, I guess I can't blame her.

I transferred to the University of Colorado, smack dab in the middle of the cycling mecca of Boulder. Lots of trails and beautiful mountain roads were just outside my apartment. A mutual friend introduced me to my roommate Tony, who moved out to Colorado from South Carolina at the same time as me. Tony was also a cyclist, a very talented and fast downhill rider. Riding with Tony took my skills to a new level, and for the first time I enjoyed the downhills as much as the uphills. As I watched him ride away from me on every downhill, my goal was to keep him in my sights a bit longer each time. I never got fast enough to keep him in sight for an entire downhill. I did, however, get a lot faster on the long Colorado downhills.

In Boulder, Tony and I ventured out on long rides each weekend, and lots of night rides during the week. Life revolved around school, bikes, work, and more bikes. The local trails - Walker Ranch, White Ranch, Golden Gate State Park, and the secret Nederland trails - became as common as the bike paths I rode to and from classes.

A group of four of us entered the 24 Hours of Moab race in 1996. I thought I drew the short straw when I got stuck with the 2:00 a.m. lap, but instead it infected me with the endurance riding bug. In the desert, on the top of a climb, there was only darkness, my handlebar lights, and a few other rider's lights that could be seen in the distance. The peacefulness of that lap will always stay with me.

Just like my first car took me away from my bike riding, my miles gradually declined after graduating from college in 1997.

My riding kicked back into high gear in 2002 when I discovered the Saturday morning rides organized by my new local shop, Bicycle Pedal'r. Ed, the owner, and Adam, the shop manager, became the new Steve and Layne. Riding every Saturday morning with a great group of riders (Dale, Chip, Scott, Brion, and many more) brought back the excitement of riding.

When I read "The Way of the Mountain Turtle" in an issue of *Dirt Rag*, where Kent Petersen documented his 2005 ride in the Great Divide Mountain Bike Race (the precursor to the Tour Divide), my riding focus changed. The world of bikepacking - riding and carrying all of your gear on the bike to sustain you for multiple days - became my new goal. I talked about various rides with Stan when I travelled back to South Carolina, dreaming of one day riding through the Rockies.

After I tested gear and setups in my backyard, my first bikepacking trip was with my then three-year-old son. With a trailer attached to my bike, we took off on a short ride to Chatfield State Park for a night of camping and plenty of time spent at the playground. For the first time, I felt the freedom and joy of being a self-contained bikepacker.

Around the same time, my friend Brion introduced me to Shawn. They both had been riding the Nebraska United Methodist Bike Ride for Hunger (NUMB), a multi-day ride in Nebraska to raise money for hunger projects. In 2009, they invited me to join them. I know, I know. Riding for several days in Nebraska is an unusual choice for a rider who enjoys climbs. It's something I pondered over and over as the three of us drove past corn field after corn field on the way to Ogalalla, in western Nebraska.

The ride ended up being a lot of fun. We had a great time on and off the bikes, hanging out with other riders in small towns in between days of riding on quiet open prairie roads. The riding was very different from the grinding climbs I was used to back in Colorado. Instead, it became quite a challenge to keep pace with the guys in aero bars that could crank out a very high speed for hours at a time. Being used to riding uphill at 8 mph and then downhill at 30+ mph, doesn't prepare you to sit in your big ring cranking on a flat road that seemingly has no end.

Six of us dialed back the speed and replaced it with stupid bike antics. Why ride in a pace line when one can sprint out of the group while yelling some corny joke for no apparent reason other than to be silly? Well, most people called it stupid so we named ourselves "Team I'm with Stupid." Greg, Em, Brion, Shawn, Chad, and myself were the charter members.

After stopping and eating at a rest stop, one of us would mount our bike, and immediately sprint away. Those left behind would look around, knowing that we had to chase the person down. Why? We had an unwritten rule - there would be no free solo escapes, and all five of us would form a cycling posse to catch the outlaw rider. Once we made the catch, another rider would dart away, repeating the process all over again. Yeah, we were stupid, but we were smiling and laughing as we rode past mile after mile of corn fields. I enjoyed the "Team I'm with Stupid" antics and people of NUMB so much, it became an annual event on my cycling calendar.

Driving back from the 2013 NUMB ride, Brion and I talked about the Tour Divide and how much I wanted to participate in the race.

"Do you really want to race it?" he asked.

"Yes! Absolutely!"

"Want to ride it together?"

From that moment on a lonely stretch of I-76 in eastern Colorado, my dream started to become reality. Brion and I were headed for the 2014 Tour Divide Race.

3

A Cold, Rainy Start

O N JUNE 13, 2014, I STOOD IN the pouring rain outside the YMCA in Banff, waiting for Crazy Larry to count down and start the 2014 Tour Divide. Nine months of training, obsessing over gear, map reading, and worry came down to this moment.

"Three..." Cleats clipped into pedals.

"Two..." Shouts of final goodbyes to family members there to see riders off.

"ONE!!!" All 150 racers pedaled away from the YMCA, the spray from the bikes in front soaking me in the process. As we headed into the trees, I heard the sound of tires on dirt. The journey was underway. My dream was a reality. I was racing the Tour Divide.

Just two days earlier, I had been a bumbling mess of tears as I said goodbye to my wife and kids at the Denver airport. Those tearful minutes of saying goodbye to my family, seeing my kids so upset at dad leaving for up to a month, were possibly the hardest part of the entire race. It was very difficult to walk away from my wife and kids, unsure of how long we would be separated.

It's easy to dream. Taking the first step to make that dream a reality is not easy at all. In fact, that's the most difficult step along the way.

I managed to compose myself enough to get through security, and that's when the alone-ness hit me. I was in an airport surrounded by people, yet I was all by myself. The only way I could get back to my family was to ride my bike 2745 miles to the finish where my dad would pick me up. Stopping in the middle of the route was not an option. At least not one I was willing to consider.

Luckily, my friend and fellow racer Nic Handy was on the same flight, and our bike talk helped ease my mind a bit. We arrived in Calgary late on Wednesday. After a dark drive to Banff, we checked into the hotel, our home base for the next thirty-six hours.

Waking up Thursday morning, the scenery was simply spectacular. I have seen a lot of mountains, but none quite as majestic as the ones surrounding Banff. After a bit of sightseeing and picture taking, we unboxed our bikes and headed out for a test ride. The Canadian mountain trails lived up to my expectations - beautiful, tacky dirt, with trees and mountains in every direction.

Our bikes and gear were setup and ready for the start the next morning. That evening we ate dinner at a local bar while Crazy Larry gave a few last minute updates, words of encouragement, and even his advice on how to handle a bear encounter. The entire room laughed at his animated, over-the-top recommendation.

Back in the hotel room, I went over my gear one final time and I began to worry about the start of the race. Would I be riding solo from the start? Would I remember what to do if I ran into a bear? Could I ride 140 miles to Starwood on the first day?

Nic, on the other hand, calmly sat on his bed packing his gear. He was experienced with solo bikepacking trips, and knew how to take things as they came instead of worrying about the unknown.

"It's almost 10:00 p.m., and it's still completely light outside," he said as he walked over to the window.

"Looks like the clouds are building. I think we're in for rain tomorrow morning," I said.

"Probably."

"What's your plan for tomorrow?" I asked. I couldn't bring myself to ask him outright if he wanted to ride together on that first day. I didn't want to interfere with his race and slow him down.

"Let's start together and see what happens."

My final check of the weather forecast confirmed the rain was moving in that night. A rainy start was almost guaranteed.

Somehow, as I lay down to sleep, all of the thoughts and worries that filled my head vanished. I drifted off to sleep, something that I would be begging for a few days later while struggling to sleep during the race.

My alarm went off at 6:00 a.m. and I opened the curtains to check the weather. Yep, it was raining, and raining hard. It seems to always rain on me when I enter a bike race. Regardless of location (Canada, Colorado, or South Carolina), my history with bike races was filled with mud and rain.

I threw on almost every layer of clothing I had packed, and covered them with rain pants and my rain jacket. The only items of clothing remaining in my seat bag were my sleep shorts and down jacket.

Riders gathered at the YMCA where the race started. Some buzzed around making last minute adjustments. Others calmly stood inside the building, avoiding the rain. I stood outside, taking in the scene of 150 riders getting ready as I got soaked by the rain. Since I was about to take off into the wet, muddy woods, I saw no point in trying to hide indoors. It turned out none of us would experience dry clothes for several days.

Since its inception in 2008, the Tour Divide "grand depart" starts in Banff on the second Friday in June. Sometimes racers enjoy dry conditions with no rain or snow. Other years, riders are greeted by remnants of the previous winter's snow at the top of the Canadian and northern Montana passes. The 2014 edition of the race held some of the wettest and snowiest conditions during the history of the Tour Divide.

At the start, I was surprisingly calm, a pleasant surprise given how nervous I had been the previous day. Maybe it was the rain, maybe it was the realization that all of the planning, analyzing, training, nervousness, and dreaming came down to this moment. Either way, I was excited to start this race.

The first few miles flew by with some riders really pushing it, others taking it easy, and a few stopping to make adjustments due to the rain and mud. Before I knew it, we reached the Spray River bridge, which had been the topic of a lot of pre-race conversations. The bridge had washed out, and a new bridge was currently under construction. Prior to the race, we wondered if we would be allowed to cross the partially rebuilt bridge, or be forced to wade through the icy cold water. With the rain falling, there were no Parks Canada or construction workers present, allowing us to use the unfinished bridge instead of fording the creek.

At the far end of the bridge, a ladder was placed to walk up the bank. While pushing my loaded sixty-pound bike up the steep embankment, I slipped several times. Luckily, I kept my balance and didn't fall back on Nic or the other riders lined up behind me.

Up next was the first real climb of the ride. It was steep and muddy, and the raindrops became bigger and fatter. That's when I realized the snow was starting to fall. For the next hour, the snow continued, covering the trail and turning the puddles into slush.

The only thing that kept running through my head was the song "Do You Want To Build a Snowman?" from the movie *Frozen*. I imagined talking to my kids and having them laugh along as I sang in the snow. I was soaked to the bone, my hands beginning to numb, but I knew there was no sense in worrying about the weather. It was what it was, and I pressed on.

Two hours into the race, I reached the Goat Creek trailhead, surprised to see Crazy Larry. He had driven to the trailhead to enthusiastically encourage us as only he can. I came through in 13th position, on Friday the 13th, with a full moon rising that night.

The snow gave way to rain, and then to intermittent rain as Nic and I navigated around Spray Lakes Reservoir. We decided to stop for a snack and try to thaw out our hands. It turned out to be a very short stop. Without pedaling to generate body heat, my entire body began to shiver. I knew I had to keep riding to stay warm.

As we continued to navigate the trails around Spray Lakes Reservoir, Nic realized he had a problem with his GPS. With so many turns and side trails, it was necessary to stop and reset the unit to resolve the issue. Nic told me to keep riding. I knew he would catch back up to me. In the first four hours of the race, the field had already spread out enough that I was riding alone. The leaders were miles ahead of me. The only person I remember seeing during this section was a woman on a singlespeed wearing all green rain gear.

I was barreling down the long downhill section just before the Mt. Shark trailhead when I heard a "whoosh" from behind. Before I could turn around, Sam and Katie raced past me on their tandem, with Katie sporting a tutu. Man, they were flying while also having a great time.

The remainder of the day turned out to be a mixture of rain, a small window of sunshine, and more rain.

Nic caught back up to me at Bolton Trading Post, sixty miles into the race. A lot of riders had stopped to take a break and recharge on the food available at the trading post.

Nic stayed there a bit longer because his knee had tightened up. I left Bolton, riding with Dan Hensley. The field had spread out again, and it was just the two of us riding over the top of Elk Pass and on towards Elkford.

"So what's your plan for the day?" I asked.

"I'm going to ride. When I get tired, I'll stop for the night," came his reply.

"That's it, you don't have a goal in mind?"

"Nope. I just ride," Dan quipped.

I wish I had more of his easy going mindset when it came to goals and plans for each day. His approach was to simply ride his bike each day. It served him well, as he ended up as the top sin-glespeed rider for 2014.

Cresting Elk Pass, I was left to imagine how spectacular the scenery would be on a clear day. I glimpsed portions of the jag-ged and rocky mountains through a few tiny breaks in the cloud clover. Dan and I caught up to three other riders. Our group of five rode at roughly the same speed along Elk River Road. Some powered quickly up the inclines while others dominated the flat sections. The rain followed intermittently as riders leap-frogged each other on the wide dirt road.

At 8:00 p.m. and 110 miles into the day, our group arrived in Elkford and headed for Kapp's Pizza. Dan, Montana Miller, Daniel Cooley, Casey Rhea, and I sat down to order hot pizza, coffee, Coke, and hot chocolate. Nic arrived a few minutes later. I was glad to see him again, and also happy that his knee wasn't bothering him too much.

As we ate, the cold day turned even colder. I went outside to get my down jacket and realized that we were in for a very cold, wet night. My goal was to ride another thirty miles to Sparwood, which would keep me on track for a twenty-one day finish. The owner of a local gym came into the restaurant while we dis-cussed our plans - should we keep riding or stay at the Elkford Motor Inn? He welcomed us all to stay at his gym two blocks away, even though the hotel had plenty of available rooms.

I decided to stay in Elkford at the gym. How could I turn down the generosity the gym owner displayed towards a bunch of soaking wet, muddy riders? It was important for me to race while also enjoying the experience - the people, places, and things that are encountered over such a long distance.

Dan and Montana decided to keep riding towards Sparwood even though it meant a cold, wet night of camping. Nic, Daniel, Casey, and I rode over to the gym. The four of us shared our stories, talked about our families, and discussed our goals for the race.

As I got ready for bed, the long, cold day caught up with me. I wrapped myself in my down quilt and closed my eyes. My first day riding the Tour Divide was officially in the books.

4

Preparation

HOW DID I GO FROM that lonely stretch of eastern Colorado interstate discussing the race with Brion to starting the race alongside Nic? It involved a lot of training rides, tons of research on the route, and a few tough conversations.

The first of those conversations involved my wife, Kristi. We had already discussed my dream of riding the Tour Divide. However, the event never made it into our family plans. With two young boys and family vacations, we could not afford the time associated with a month long race.

When Brion and I returned home, I seem to recall me telling my wife "Hey, Brion wants to ride the Tour Divide. Wouldn't it be great if we could ride it together?"

Her version is a bit different. She recalls me saying "Brion and I decided to do the Tour Divide. I only have nine months to get ready, so I will need to spend a lot of time training."

Her memory is much better than mine so her version is likely the truth. There was no family sit-down to discuss if the Tour Divide would work out. There was no discussion of how I could manage weeks off from work. I didn't leave the decision to debate. I just knew I was committed to the race and would make it happen. Thankfully, Kristi was understanding of my desire to complete my dream ride, even with my lousy way of bringing up the subject. (Sorry, Kristi. But at least we got to work on this book together!)

My local bike shop, Alpha Bicycle Company, carried my dream bike - the Moots YBB. The large 29" wheels and titanium frame with just enough suspension to take the edge off of long days in the saddle (while not adding too much weight to the bike) made the perfect build to tackle the Tour Divide.

Nic Handy was the head mechanic at Alpha, and planned to race the Tour Divide himself in 2015. He meticulously built my bike part by part, producing the finest mechanic work I have ever seen. Even the smallest detail received his complete focus. During the hours while we discussed bike parts and bikepacking gear, Nic became a good friend. His planned 2015 Tour Divide was moved up a year to join Brion and me in 2014.

My training plan was simple - ride my bike as much as I could with a little bit of running mixed in.

The remainder of 2013 was filled with lots of bike riding. Brion and I were both excited and we kept riding more miles each month. Even when the Colorado weather turned cold in the fall, the miles kept rolling by.

With a full time job, a family, and other obligations, I couldn't ride every day. Some days were a quick hour ride at lunch. Others were what I consider one of the worst forms of exercise known to man, a thirty-minute run on the treadmill. Instead of watching Denver Broncos games, I rode for several hours, making it back in time to catch the end of the fourth quarter. As the start of the Tour Divide approached, my week-end rides turned into six-, eight-, and ten-hour rides.

Riding my bike was the easy part. I knew how to throw my legs over the bike and pedal. In the year leading up to the race, I put in more miles in more types of weather than ever before. Physically, I was as ready as I could be. I needed to work on details - gear, food, and route planning.

The engineering side of my brain wanted to control the variables. What was the optimal method of storing gear on my bike? What items could I cut from my packing list to be more light-weight? Could I make specialized gear to serve my Tour Divide needs instead of compromising on what I found in the store?

I packed, re-packed, and then packed my gear again, looking for the most efficient method. My gear was weighed and entered into a spreadsheet to help me evenly distribute the weight on my bike. Every piece of gear was scrutinized. I considered all kinds of questions - did I need to carry two spare tubes? Could I get by with only a bivy sack and no tarp or tent? Could I wear one pair of shorts for the entire ride? Did I need to carry any patches to repair my sleeping pad? What if I carried 12" of emergency duct tape instead of 18"? I was obsessed with shaving ounces, reducing the bulk of my items, and coming up with the optimal gear kit for my race.

I even went so far as to make my own cuben fiber rain socks. This involved hours of researching vapor barrier clothing, making a template, and then putting the socks together multiple times since my first attempt made them too small. All of this was in the name of a lightweight pair of socks that ended up not working very well.

In the end, I settled on the following gear for my race:

- Ultralight tarp and bivy for my shelter
- Down quilt instead of a down sleeping bag
- A full sized sleeping pad and inflatable pillow
- No spare riding clothes - only a spare pair of socks
- Fairly comprehensive first aid kit
- Minimal gear repair kit
- A small razor blade instead of a knife
- One set of backup batteries
- Tiny emergency blanket and emergency light

In addition to the optimizing of my gear, I spent countless hours poring over the Adventure Cycling Association (ACA) maps for the route. This work included the development of a day-by-day best case, average case, and worst case schedule. I read multiple books about other rider's adventures during the Tour Divide. Google Maps became my friend as I researched towns and road conditions. I used my Garmin software to make detailed notes on elevation gain between various checkpoints. My plan was to know ahead of time where I could re-supply and how much climbing was required between locations.

The hours I spent on gear selection and route planning definitely paid off when it came to the race. I didn't have to think about where to pack items on my bike, or spend brain power to find resources, or know where the towns were along the route.

As winter turned to spring, my training shifted to riding almost exclusively with a fully loaded bike to get used to the weight. I needed to get used to a fifty-pound bike instead of a twenty-five pound bike. My goals for the spring centered around three big rides - the 170 mile Anti-Epic (a gravel grinder in eastern Colorado), a three day trip on the Kokopelli Trail between Fruita, CO and Moab, UT, and finally, a three day ride on the Colorado Trail that started twenty-miles from my house.

Up first was the Anti-Epic in early April. A very cold start gave way to a comfortable morning of riding as Brion and I tested out gear, bike setups, and food choices.

Around the forty-mile mark, I was riding with a couple of other guys and we were chatting about whether we were training for something else like the Dirty Kanza 200 or other races. When I mentioned that I was doing the Tour Divide, one of the guys introduced himself as Nic Legan. I knew his name from his MTBCast call-ins during the 2013 race. (MTBCast is a free service that allows riders to call in as they ride the Tour Divide to post voicemail updates and keep listeners informed on the race and their progress.)

We pedaled down the quiet country roads with small inclines as we talked about my preparations and goals for the race. Nic was very open, as most bikepackers are, about what worked and didn't work during his attempt at the 2013 race. Ultimately, his sore Achilles forced him to drop out in Wyoming.

Nic's best advice was about how to finish each day. Instead of finishing in a town, he suggested the idea of re-supplying in a town and then riding for another hour or two at a very slow pace. The reason for this is twofold - don't get stuck in towns too long, and make extra miles each day that will add up over the course of three weeks.

On my training rides following the Anti-Epic, I focused on my nutrition. The Tour Divide required a high calorie diet, and most food along the route would come from gas stations. Hostess Fruit Pies, Snickers bars, and candy orange slices became my go-to fuel during long rides. Did you know that a Hostess Fruit Pie has almost 500 calories in that mess of chemicals, dough, and fake filling? Hey, it was all about easy calories, not wholesome food.

Later in April, I joined Nic Handy and several other riders on a Colorado Trail bikepacking trip. Due to family commitments, I had to turn around early on the second day. Riding solo through the mountains as day faded into darkness forced me to practice solo night riding, something I had neglected to address during my previous training rides.

The final shakedown before the trip to Banff was a planned three day trip on the Kokopelli trail in mid-May with Brion. As we unloaded the car and started riding away from Fruita, the heat was stifling. Yes, I know we were in the desert. But in mid-May, it wasn't supposed to be in the high 90s. We made slow progress on that first day.

Heat was still an issue the second day. Even Brion, who usually only takes a couple of drinks of water during a long ride, was quickly depleting his water supplies. We filled up at the ranger station on the Colorado River before heading out to ride over more sand and rocks. For a long stretch, the trail stayed close to the Colorado River, offering views from high on the hills and occasionally dropping down to almost river level. While we generally ride at the same pace on long rides, Brion was struggling with the heat and terrain. Instead of pushing further into the desert, we bailed on the Kokopelli and rode the fifty miles of pavement back to our vehicle.

Back in Fruita, over a well-deserved meal, Brion was wiped out. He is normally a man of very few words. At that meal, I think he said a total of ten words. I knew his mind and body were not in a good place. A few days later, he let me know that he was pulling out of the Tour Divide, a tough decision for him to reach. Due to a combination of work and family obligations, Brion had not been able to dedicate enough time to train for the race.

While I would miss sharing this adventure with Brion, I completely understood and respected his decision. Even though he wasn't there with me physically, Brion continued to play an important part in my Tour Divide adventure. During the race, he sent me a daily text message containing an inspirational quote. (Coincidentally, his quote always reflected the conditions and challenges I encountered that day.) I was grateful to have someone like him to call my friend. Without his prodding, I would not have been on the path to the 2014 Tour Divide.

With less than a month left to train, my legs were stronger than ever. My gear was selected and organized. The re-supply points and mileages of the route were etched into my brain. But my mindset needed to change. The safety net of racing with a friend and riding companion had disappeared. I didn't expect to match Nic's riding pace, and I knew he wanted to ride his own ride. Mentally, I needed to prepare myself for riding the race alone.

5

Digging Deep in the Mud

W E WOKE UP TO A light mist which soon turned to a drizzle. The second day turned out to be a 160 mile slog from Elkford to Eureka, Montana, riding over three passes and through the Flathead Valley - the longest ride of my life, fully loaded, in the rain.

Why was Eureka my goal for that day? First, it meant re-supply, hot food, and the ever-important hot coffee the next morning. Second, I would get through the two maps of the Canadian section in two days, keeping me on pace to finish in twenty-one days. Third, I wanted to avoid camping in the Flathead Valley, if at all possible, because of the high concentration of grizzlies.

I allowed my anxiety around camping in grizzly country to cloud my judgement. Pushing myself beyond my limits this early had repercussions for the remainder of the race.

With hindsight, I realize the push for the U.S. Border was a mistake from a physical perspective. Riding 160 miles with the extra effort of pedaling through the rain and mud brought on the dreaded Achilles pain that so many Tour Divide riders experience. I don't know if the soreness and searing pain would have occurred later in the race. The huge push on the second day certainly created it, and the pain became something that would bother me for the remainder of the race.

Before leaving Elkford, British Columbia, I left my first MTBCast update. The call-ins provided my friends and family a glimpse into the adventure and my progress. The first update centered around rain, snow, excitement, and cold. Based on the light mist falling in Elkford, the second day appeared to be similar riding conditions.

Our group of four left town at 5:30 a.m. The first few miles went up a steep paved road on the way to the local mine, providing a nice warmup to the chilly morning before we turned on the new-for-2014 re-route to Sparwood, British Columbia. While the new route had a few bits of singletrack trails, it was mostly doubletrack trails, which were fun to ride in the mud and the drizzle. After this section, we rode dirt roads for a few miles and then finished on pavement as we made our way into Sparwood to load up on breakfast, coffee, and supplies for the rest of the day.

While paying for my breakfast at the A&W, I saw in my wallet the note that my seven-year-old son had written for me a few days before I left for the race. It read:

"Have a great ride on the tour divide!!!
Just for you!!!!!!!!!!
Love, your youngest son."

It gave me the inspiration I needed to keep pushing for the border on a day that I knew would be the longest and hardest of my cycling career. Throughout the race, I saw that note each time I pulled out a credit card to pay for food.

After Sparwood, there is a thirty-mile section of pavement that gently climbs up to the base of Flathead Pass. Casey and I were riding together at this point, companions in our effort to reach the U.S. border. The climb up Flathead Pass was pleasant and it felt good to be climbing into the mountains, especially since the rain had stopped. Little did we know how wet we were going to be over the next few hours!

The ACA maps state that "you will get wet" on the downhill of Flathead Pass. I was expecting a few areas of runoff and maybe a creek crossing or two. Initially, that's exactly what we found. At the first creek crossing, we unsuccessfully tried to find a way across without getting our feet soaked. Soon after that first crossing, the creek and road merged into one - the icy snowmelt completely covering the road. There was no way to avoid the stream of water, and my feet quickly became soaked and numb. Instead of trying to find good lines, I took the shortest path, plunging into the water time and time again.

The downhill eventually flattened out, and we continued to ride through large puddles of water covering the entire path until we reached forest service roads. The skies opened up and the rain once again started falling. Casey and I put our heads down and pushed toward Butts Cabin, where we planned to stop for a lunch break. Along the way, we encountered a moose that did not want to leave the road, forcing us to stop and wait until he moved. By this point I could barely feel my fingers and toes, a direct result of riding in the constant, chilly rain. Finally, we rounded the corner and found Butt's Cabin (an old one-room cabin in the middle of the woods) with a warm fire blazing out front.

The fire was the most beautiful, welcoming sight, and the sun even poked out for a few minutes while we were there. While I dried out my rain gear, gloves, and feet, I chatted with the people who were camping out next to the cabin. They were there for a birthday weekend of bear hunting. Needless to say, they were very interested to know if we had seen any bears. There's nothing like talking to bear hunters in grizzly country when you're already nervous about bears to give you the extra drive to keep on riding.

We left Butt's Cabin with dry clothes and our stomachs full. Ten minutes later, as we started up Cabin Pass, it was raining, but those few dry minutes were enjoyable. This became the theme for the remainder of the day. Just when we began to dry out, the rain started up again. After climbing up Cabin Pass, we bombed down a very fun downhill and made our way to the notorious connector trail.

Pictures don't do this trail justice. The trail is so steep, riders are forced to dismount and walk their bike to the top. It feels like climbing up a vertical wall, all while struggling with a sixty-pound bike. And to make matters worse, we had to do it in the mud and the rain. The technique I employed to make it to the top wasn't pretty: push the bike forward a few feet, grab the brakes, and then try to walk a few steps without sliding down. Repeat.

The twenty minutes of pushing felt like two hours. My arms and shoulders burned from the effort to move forward. I kept pushing until the trail opened into a small clearing and the start of my last climb of the day - Galton Pass. From my pre-race research, I knew Galton Pass had a profile like a perfect triangle -

no false flats with steep grades on the uphill and downhill. The promise of a fast downhill motivated me as I started to climb.

Darkness fell as we slowly made our way up Galton. As I rode, it got steeper and steeper. That's when I decided to walk the first of many climbs during the race. In the dark night, I relied on my head light as I alternately walked and pedaled my way through the upper switchbacks. The light rain continued to fall. Finally, the GPS showed the top of the climb.

It was around 10:00 p.m. when Casey and I crested the top of Galton Pass.

"This is going to be a cold downhill," I said as I put on extra layers.

"Last one of the day," Casey replied.

"I've been looking forward to this one. It's supposed to be steep and fast."

"With my lights, I can't see very well. I need to go slow," Casey said.

"Ok, be safe and I'll see you at the border," I said as I zipped up my jacket and clicked into my pedals.

I love night riding, and I love downhills. This combination led me to the edge of insanity as I flew down the road, carrying too much speed around the corners. Given my weariness from riding 140+ miles that day, the wet ground, and the unknown terrain that lie ahead, I should have been more cautious. But I wanted to get to the bottom and to the border. The cold air kept me alert while I barreled into the darkness.

6

Night Riding

AS I SPED DOWN GALTON PASS at a rate that was too fast for the dark and rainy conditions, I was brought back to all of the nights I spent night riding over the last twenty years. From the very first night ride with Stan in South Carolina to my latest training rides on the Colorado Trail just a month earlier, they were all helping me reach my goal of making it to the U.S. border.

For me, there is something calming about riding a mountain bike with just my light illuminating a small patch of the trail in front of me. Other distractions fall away, while my focus and concentration is needed to ensure I stay on the trail. There is nothing to look at but darkness. No vistas, mountain views, or peeking at the trail ahead.

Go too fast, and a crash is inevitable. It's one thing to bomb down a mountain that you have ridden many times during the day. It's another to fly down an unfamiliar mountain, completely unaware of what's up ahead, with a light rain falling, after 140 miles of riding for the day. All sane thoughts told me to take it slower. All of my crazy thoughts told me to keep going. After all, I had earned a "fun" downhill after struggling to get to the top of Galton Pass. Not to mention I was cold and anxious to get to the U.S. border.

I was laser-focused on the road in front of me, as I rode stupid-fast at the edge of my abilities. I had to make sure I didn't go over it. That balance of riding on the edge is another draw of night riding.

I'll admit that my first few night rides back in South Carolina didn't bring these same enduring thoughts. Stan and I headed out on some trails near my parent's house. It was a struggle to adjust to not seeing the trail up ahead. Your field of vision goes from hundreds of feet in daylight to a small sphere of ten feet at night. On more than one occasion that night, turns in the trail came completely by surprise, and I found myself off in the woods on pine straw rather than on the path of the trail. Over time and after quite a bit of practice, I learned to embrace the uncertainty of navigating in the dark and found the required focus. I became hooked on night riding.

Two other friends and I travelled to Fontana, North Carolina to race the 12 Hours Of Mud Puppy. I happily took the first night lap. As I was out on course riding next to a small creek, a bird flew in the beam of my lights. It stayed with me for what seemed like a mile or more. In reality, it was probably only for a hundred yards. I still remember that moment vividly in my mind. It wasn't the fact that I saw a bird as I was night riding; rather it was the moment when I was one with the night and the bird. The world was perfectly aligned with rider, environment, and animals moving at the same pace. Everything else disappeared for those few brief seconds.

We can ride for years and years and only have a couple of these moments when everything aligns and it just feels right.

The world is quiet, the body doesn't feel the pedaling, the surroundings embrace us, and the rhythm of the world moves at the same beat.

Upon moving to Boulder, Colorado, I branched out and did even more night riding. There was a weekly night ride leaving from the Full Cycle bike shop. We would ride a variety of local trails (Logan Mill/Betasso, Chataqua, Golden Gate, White Ranch, Walker Ranch). This is where my night riding skills got much better. It's also where I learned to be more comfortable with "the eyes." At night, when you stop for a break and shine your headlight into the surrounding woods, you often see glowing eyes. Some are small, some are larger. Some even encourage you to not be the last person in the group for the next section.

More than likely, they are all non-threatening animals like raccoons or deer. However, there were probably times where the eyes were connected to a mountain lion or bobcat. It's kind of like the bears on the Tour Divide. You know they are around and you are watchful for their signs, but you can't dwell on the fact they are present. Be aware and keep on riding.

One of my final night time training rides before flying up to Calgary was a long stretch on the Colorado Trail. Nic organized a two night beginner's bikepacking trip to get more people out on the trails. Due to a family commitment I couldn't stay for the second night. To get in a long fully-loaded training ride, I rode with the group until mid-afternoon on the second day. At that point, I turned around and rode solo for the remainder of the day and night, returning home well after dark. My day's total was eighty miles on terrain more technical and challenging than the Tour Divide.

After being with a group for almost two days, it was strange to ride solo through areas where the chance of running into other riders was slim. As night started to fall, I was riding down Section 2 on my way towards Waterton Canyon. It's a familiar trail for me, although one I had never ridden at night. The fatigue from a long day of grinding up hills in my easiest gears faded away. It was me and my light beam riding through some wonderful Colorado singletrack.

As my route home took me to the end of the Colorado Trail, through the Chatfield State Park roads, and back into the metro Denver area, I stopped at a gas station for a quick Coke and snack. While sitting on a bench and consuming my sugar and caffeine, I made a quick call to my wife to let her know my ETA. To take a line from the Eagles, I enjoyed the peaceful easy feeling that comes from reaching the end of a bikepacking trip in the mountains.

Back in Canada, I was on my second day of what would be a much longer bikepacking trip, barreling down the mountains towards the pavement that would take me to the US border and Eureka, Montana on the other side. While it wasn't quite comparable to sipping a Coke, calling my wife, and having a comfortable bed waiting at home, it was satisfying knowing that I was riding through the night and out of the woods.

The terrain, fear of bears, and distance from home were unfamiliar. In the end, it was just another night ride. All I could see was the small spot of Earth illuminated by my headlight. Keep pedaling and eventually the dirt turns to pavement and the pavement leads to civilization.

7

Overextended and Exhausted

THE DOWNHILL DUMPED OUT ONTO pavement providing me with easy cruising in the final miles to the U.S. border. There was one moment of panic when the road sign listed the distance to the border as "15." Then I remembered I was still in Canada, and the signs were in kilometers. It was fifteen kilometers - only nine miles to the border.

Whew, I could relax and cruise into Eureka. *I'm going to make it to the border!*

After a quick inspection of my passport at the crossing, I pedaled over to the First & Last Chance Bar. It was midnight, but the place was full of Tour Divide riders worn out from the long, cold day. I ordered a hot chocolate and nachos from the limited late night menu. As I sat at the bar cradling the hot chocolate in my hands, Casey walked in. I was happy to see him and to know that he safely made it down Galton Pass.

After finishing our food, Casey and I rode the ten miles to Eureka where we arrived at a hotel just behind Dan Hensley and a few others. It was 1:00 a.m. and I just wanted to lay down and sleep for the night. The woman at the front desk said that Dan's group had taken the last room. Those words stung. It was late. I had just ridden the longest ride of my life. I was tired. I was worn out.

She gave us an option, allowing us to sleep on the floor in the lounge. There was plenty of space to lay out sleeping bags. However, the only caveat was that we had to be out by 6:00 a.m. If I passed on the hotel, I could camp in the cold, wet campground behind the hotel, or continue to ride into the night and camp on the side of the road. Casey and I didn't hesitate to take the offer of the lounge.

For some reason, I had it in my head that I needed a shower that night. I don't really know why, other than I was still very new to this multi-day racing thing and felt like I needed to get clean after riding through so much water and mud that day. Instead of sleeping in my dirty clothes, I walked down to the campground and used their showers to wash myself and my completely filthy cycling clothes. It felt great to stand under the hot water after being so cold throughout the day.

After changing into dry sleep clothes and hanging my wet clothes on chairs and on the floor, I laid down to sleep. It was nearing 2:00 a.m. by this time, but I was now wide awake and unable to sleep. The rest of that night, riders continued to pour into the lounge to take refuge in any corner or open spot of carpet they could find. Each time I got close to sleep, another rider opened the door and proceeded to rustle their clothes and sleeping gear as they laid down. On top of that, there was a woman playing video poker late into the night. The beeps and sounds of the machine felt like they were right next to my ear.

In hindsight, the best decision that night would have been to set up my tarp in the wet conditions and sleep outside. I'd been backpacking quite a few times, and had a camping home that worked for me. I would have had my own space, and would have been free from the noises and riders that came into the hotel throughout the night. It was also a rookie mistake to take a shower at such a late time. I could have used the extra time to sleep, and I would just be getting dirty again the next day.

I may have dozed off a time or two, never getting into real sleep. Riders trickled in all night. At 3:00 a.m., a woman in green rain gear came into the lobby. Leaving her rain gear on, she curled into a ball on the bare floor and fell asleep, exhausted.

At 5:20 a.m. (yes, I remember the exact time), the front desk clerk began waking us up. When she said we had to be out by 6:00 a.m., she meant completely out of the hotel lobby area. That meant she was, as gently as possible, waking us up with plenty of time to get packed up and out of the hotel.

There were at least fifteen riders in the lounge the next morning when I finally rolled out of my bag. We were a rough, haggard looking crowd, trying to rouse ourselves awake after such a brutal, long day in the Flathead. A few riders decided to stay and sleep for a few more hours once a room became available. I was preparing to ride up and over both Whitefish Divide and Red Meadow Pass. As long as I could find some coffee in town.

The clothes I washed out the night before were still wet when I put them on that morning. The previous night, I failed to register the fact that clothes don't dry in a few hours when it's humid and raining outside. I wanted to find breakfast and coffee to put the miserable night behind me. I quickly learned that looking forward to a hot meal in the cafe is a sure way to have your hopes dashed on the Tour Divide. It was Sunday morning and the cafe didn't open until 8:00 a.m. A gas station breakfast was my only option - hot coffee, frozen sausage biscuits, and a microwave. Not quite the cafe meal I was hoping for.

Without sleep, my senses were dull, and I didn't realize how much time Casey and I spent at the gas station. We left after an hour, riding into an overcast sky that held the certainty of more rain for the day.

The route travelled southeast on paved roads. A left turn crossed over Highway 93 and onto the road that leads over Whitefish Divide. Like the Canadian section, the scenery in this area was something I looked forward to experiencing. And just like the Canadian section, all I saw were low grey clouds with an occasional break offering a glimpse of the peaks. The road narrowed as it climbed up toward the divide, turning into dirt as the dense tree cover closed in on all sides. Even after the previous day's long ride and minimal sleep, my legs felt strong. I rode ahead of Casey, climbing alone through the trees and the light mist that began to fall.

When a year has normal snowfall (and 2014 had plenty), snow still exists at the top of Whitefish Divide in the month of June. The unknown was where the snow would start and how much remained. The answer came quickly and a long, long way from the summit. A strong pine aroma filled the air as I pedaled through the forest. Then I saw the source of the pine smell - a pile of avalanche debris and snow ten feet high covering the mountainside and the entire road. Shredded, twisted trees and pine boughs embedded in the snow made for a wonderful smell, but a terrible obstacle for a bike rider.

This was going to be a year of epic bike pushing through the snow and debris. It was going to be a long, slow-moving day.

I had to figure out a way to get myself and my bike up and over the tangled mess. My technique started out fairly simple. I stepped up on the snow pile, and pushed my bike until I reached a limb or tree trunk blocking my way. I lifted my bike over the obstruction, and then I stepped over it while trying to prevent the bike from sliding back onto me.

As I climbed Whitefish Divide, I found myself in an obstacle course of avalanche debris. I climbed between, over, and under trees and limbs as I maneuvered my fully loaded bike through the tight openings in the debris. Some debris piled up to twenty feet high, other sections were as long as a football field, and some were littered with entire trees embedded in the snow; sometimes it was a combination of all three. It was a relief to hit a section that was only a few feet high - nothing more than a pile of snow with a well-worn path over the top.

The only constants were the snow and the aroma of the pine trees. The trees had been broken apart, which opened their fragrant sap and needles. It was a wonderful smell, like a car freshener on steroids. Now, every time I smell a pine tree, I'm transported back to this moment on the Tour Divide.

As I worked my way across the initial debris fields, the humor of the situation kept me smiling. Then the cold feet, the light rain, and the tired arms settled in. Misery and frustration replaced the humor as my pace dropped to less than 4 mph. I managed to catch three New Zealand riders towards the top, and we shared in the suffering.

After cresting the top of Whitefish Divide, the debris fields continued and progress remained slow. The intense pine scent permeated the air. I rode short sections before dismounting and walking over more trees. Further down the mountain, the snow and avalanche debris finally disappeared. Without obstacles, I quickly descended ahead of the New Zealand riders to the bottom where the road leveled out. I caught back up to Dan on the flatter road. We rode together for an hour before I took advantage of a break in the rain to stop for lunch.

Across the road was the North Fork Flathead River. Beyond the river, the majestic mountains of Glacier National Park rose up from the valley. Oh, how I wish the skies had been clear to let me experience the amazing views instead of the low cloud cover blanketing the landscape.

Sitting down gave me a chance to eat more of my gas station food and recharge before climbing up Red Meadow Pass. With an elevation 500 feet higher than Whitefish Divide, I expected to find even more snow on Red Meadow Pass. While pondering more bike pushing, I noticed that my brand new toe warmers were shredded on the bottom. In less than three days, the Tour Divide destroyed them. Now they barely stayed in place on my shoes.

The New Zealand riders leap frogged me once again as I adjusted my toe warmers and packed up my food.

I rode alone down the dirt road after lunch. As the road turned uphill, I began to struggle. The hard riding from the day before caused a lot of soreness in both Achilles. I believe it was caused by riding for miles through the muddy roads in the Flathead with my heel pointed down for extra power to push through the wheel-gripping mud. The pushing and climbing over steep snow banks on Whitefish Divide only made the soreness worse.

I decided to pull out my iPod and listen to my "inspire" playlist. Before the ride, I told myself to only use the headphones when absolutely necessary because I wanted to experience the ride and nature as completely as I could. This was my first of only four brief times I used the headphones.

An hour later, my riding came to an abrupt stop. I rounded a corner and was met by a three foot wall of snow. The snow covered the road and the forest in all directions. I was more than two miles from the top of the pass. I dismounted and began to walk.

With each step, I measured my stride to land in the holes created by those riders ahead of me. It was easier to high step into the existing holes than break new tracks through the soft crust of the snow. I entered a trance-like state as the minutes turned into an hour. My only reminder of distance was the ever-increasing burning sensation in my arms from constantly pushing my bike.

As I walked, I caught back up to the New Zealanders. It was nice to have other riders around during this section of very slow bike pushing. We continued to follow the footprints in the snow. Jefe Branham, the race leader, would have encountered a pristine blanket of white snow. I can't imagine how long it must have taken him to cross this pass.

"This is fun, huh?" I said to them.

"Oh yeah, loving it," came the sarcastic reply.

With the snow on the ground, the low clouds, and the light rain that had returned, the world was reduced to a white haze. Depth perception was lost. We could only make out faint shapes in the distance.

I said, "All we need now is a grizzly walking beside us to make this even more crazy."

"Yeah, that would be just perfect."

Fortunately, the grizzlies didn't hear this and never made an appearance.

After passing Red Meadow Lake at the top of the climb, we began to descend, still walking through several feet of snow. It was like a snowshoe hike, minus the snowshoes. Eventually, we found the end of the snow pack and stepped onto dirt for the first time in over an hour. The four of us pedaled down the mountain only to be stopped by another patch of snow covering the entire road. This sequence of riding then climbing over more snow repeated itself multiple times. My frustration level increased with each stop. I wanted to enjoy a fast downhill.

As we descended below 5000 feet, the snow disappeared, and I finally had the downhill I had been craving. That was the good news. The bad news? Two hours of trudging through snow and rain chilled me to my core. The cold wind from speeding downhill pushed that cold deeper and deeper into my body. In addition, my shredded toe warmers provided no insulation and my waterproof gloves were no longer waterproof. My entire three-layer glove system relied on this outer glove to stay dry. In all my meticulous planning, I had not counted on these equipment failures.

The New Zealanders pulled away from me on the downhill. All three of them had heavy gloves and waterproof socks keeping them warm. Two of the New Zealand riders would go on to finish in the top ten. I would see the third rider, Ken Scott (Scotty), again in Montana, and also much later in Colorado.

With my gloves and toe warmers failing, I could not warm up as I sped down the hill. At least I was riding and no longer walking through snow. The descent turned to pavement on the shores of Whitefish Lake. Once again, the grey sky denied me of my view, a common theme for the first three days of the race.

The road followed the edge of the lake as it made its way into town. My core temperature continued to drop, and it felt like my rain jacket had soaked through. (Little did I know, it would actually soak through two days later on Richmond Pass.) Yesterday's ride combined with little sleep and then another exhausting day had wiped me out. My body didn't even have energy to keep me warm, even though I was pedaling and trying to generate more heat.

I originally planned to ride on to Columbia Falls. However, I decided to call it a night in Whitefish, ten miles from my scheduled stop. The combination of the cold and my sore Achilles were too much. I was ready to end this brutally hard ninety-mile day.

"Andy! Andy!" I heard a voice yell as I entered town. It was Dan outside of a BBQ restaurant with several other riders.

I waved to them as I rode slowly by. "Hey Dan, you guys doing good?"

"Come on over and eat with us," he said.

"Thanks, but I'm headed to a hotel."

"Ok, good luck. See you on the road again," Dan said.

Looking back, I should have stopped to eat with the other riders. In that moment, I was focused on finding a hotel room so I could settle down and ice my Achilles. The camaraderie of my fellow riders as we shared a meal together would have made me feel better than sitting alone in my hotel room. I also wish I had stayed since it turned out to be the last time I crossed paths with Dan during the race.

Whitefish is one of those Tour Divide towns that's big enough to require navigation. You can't simply look down the main drag and see the restaurant, hotel, and gas station all within a few hundred feet. Rather than roaming around town, I stopped to ask a family if they knew of any hotels downtown. They pointed me in the right direction. A few minutes later I was checked into a hotel for the night.

Next up was food. Unfortunately, the burrito restaurant next to the hotel was closed. I hobbled to the next closest place, a sandwich shop just a few blocks away.

With my bag of food in my hand, I moseyed back to the hotel where I set about eating, drying out my gear, and making a call to my family. While talking with my wife, I realized all of the mud, snow, and grit had caused the zipper on my frame bag to get stuck. Not good.

Of course, being the guy that was worried about what was next, I became agitated with this possible issue and turned into the cranky husband unable to spend a few minutes talking with my wife and kids. I convinced myself the zipper was a major issue. I also convinced myself that since I was racing, I couldn't spend time doing non-racing things like talking on the phone. It sounds silly to write those words, but that is the way I felt that evening.

In a panic, I emailed my friend Joe Tonsager for tips on solving the zipper issues. He is the owner of J. Paks, and he custom-made all of my bikepacking bags. His advice to use chain lube and my chain-cleaning toothbrush had the zipper functioning properly within a few minutes.

With that problem solved, I had a chance to ice my Achilles. While walking through the lobby to the ice machine, I saw another Tour Divide rider trying to get a room. His credit cards were not working in the U.S.

In my mind, I was saying "Crap, crap, crap! I just want to ice my ankles and go to sleep. I don't want to talk to anyone or deal with anyone else's problems." At the same time, I knew I had to help this guy because it was the right thing to do. He had been through the same brutal day as me. I couldn't sneak through the lobby and leave him without a room.

Stephan was from Belgium. He was a super friendly guy. A super talkative guy. My room was a double, and I offered to share with him. I told him not to worry about paying his half of the room since his credit cards were not working. Inside the room, we both had gear, food, and clothes spread out. Somehow, Stephan seemed to keep pulling out more gear. It was as if he had a magic backpack that was bigger on the inside. Kind of like the TARDIS from *Doctor Who.*

While he made hot chocolate in the room, Stephan told me stories of riding in Belgium and his plans to ride the Colorado Trail after finishing the Tour Divide. At 10:00 p.m., I finally laid down and fell into a deep sleep.

The next morning, I was feeling better energy-wise, although both of my Achilles were very swollen. Each step around the hotel room that morning was very painful. I didn't have many choices - either accept the fact that the soreness was there to stay or quit riding. I certainly wasn't going to let a sore Achilles stop me. Especially when Columbia Falls, Holland Lake, and Ovando in beautiful Montana were calling my name.

I packed up my gear, ready to ride the ten miles to Columbia Falls. Stephan was still packing all of his supplies, clothes, food, and other items he had taken out the night before. Instead of waiting for Stephan, I left the key with him and carried my bike down the stairs and onto the quiet streets of Whitefish. Part of me felt bad riding off alone without Stephan and his stories to keep me company. But I knew that I needed the quiet time on the road to get my head straight and figure out how to deal with the sore Achilles problem. The previous night's rest and ice had not helped like I thought it would.

The town was quickly behind me as I pedaled past farms set away from the road and horses walking in the early morning dew. It was a peaceful morning on the outside. On the inside, I worried over how much worse my Achilles pain would get while riding more than 100 miles a day.

8

I Got This

WHEN PLANNING MY RACE ON paper, a twenty-one day finish seemed difficult but attainable. Before arriving in Banff, I carefully charted and plotted an ideal plan for each day of the race, providing milestones to keep me on track for my aggressive goal. Now, for the fourth day in a row, I faced unpredictable wet and rainy conditions. To stay on track, I'd need to travel 170 miles to finish the day in Ovando, Montana. Add to that my extremely sore Achilles, and I knew my dream of a twenty-one day finish was far out of reach. The exact finish date was no longer important. Now the key was to keep pedaling, figure out some way to manage the pain, and continue moving forward.

My thoughts kept drifting back to a phrase my youngest son began using when he was five years old.

"I got this!"

Those words are heard a lot around my house. "Hey LL, do you want me to help you with picking that up?"

"No, I got this."

"Hey LL, do you want me to help you hike up this rocky ledge?"

"No, I got this."

He is one very strong-willed child, and he doesn't let anything get in his way, regardless of how big, or scary, or heavy it might be.

When he first started riding his bike with training wheels around our hilly neighborhood, he would fly down the hills and then push as hard as his little legs could to pedal back uphill. He had to do it by himself, a push from Dad was out of the question. I was not allowed to interfere. "I got this Dad! I got this!" was always the reply whenever I asked if he needed help pedaling up those hills.

While not as vocal as his younger brother, my older son enjoys pushing his limits from time to time when I come up with crazy adventures. When he was six, we set out for our first bikepacking overnighter on the rocky singletrack of the Colorado Trail. We attached a tag-a-long to my bike, and we struggled up the steep climbs and tight switchbacks. Even with the falls and lots of walking, he kept pedaling. Our journey back the next morning allowed us to ride the downhill that gave us so much trouble the day before. Along the way, we met several Colorado Trail racers who offered words of encouragement to my son for attempting such a tough trail.

My kids' experiences motivated me that cool, misty morning as I rode gingerly past farms and horses in their pastures.

I got this.

This race was not supposed to be easy. Every day you walk a fine line between pushing yourself to your limits and not giving it everything you've got. Sticking with my plan to reach the U.S. border on the second day proved too much for my body to handle. There was nothing I could do about it now. I could only look forward. How would I overcome the physical pain, preventing it from affecting my mental state or derailing me even further?

I got this.

In any situation, there are ups and downs. It's how we manage the down times that determine the overall outcome. Coming into the race, I knew this was a one-time deal. When you think of the Tour Divide, it sounds like a month long absence from your family. What you don't think about are all the things you miss during your training in the year leading up to the race. With two young boys, I knew I could not commit to the Tour Divide again.

Pushing myself until I broke was a decision I made before the start. When I wrestled in high school, I pushed myself too hard and ended up suffering for over a year, lacking the ability to do anything that required a high level of exertion. Over twenty years later, I was willing to do the same thing again if needed, in order to get through the Tour Divide.

I got this.

And really, that whole Achilles tendon is nothing more than a narrow strip of tissue around the foot, right? That's not enough to stop me. More importantly, I needed to persevere so that in the future I can tell my kids, "You got this," whenever they come face to face with a challenge.

Before setting out on the Tour Divide, I told myself that quitting was not an option. It would take a broken leg or some other major medical issue to get me out. This was my one shot at the race, and I didn't want to waste it.

I got this.

My resolve would be tested in the next two days more than it was at any other point in the race. The weather and terrain were about to unleash their fury on me and the other riders on the 300 mile section between Columbia Falls and Helena.

9

Shivering in the Snow

OLUMBIA FALLS, I SURE HOPE you have coffee. This
thought repeated as I pedaled in the cool morning air.

The train tracks signaled the outskirts of Columbia
Falls, Montana. This meant breakfast, re-supply, and a
chance to get some better gloves for the inevitable rain that
would be falling from the dark skies overhead.

As I hit town around 8:00 a.m., a few patches of blue sky appeared between the clouds. I had worked out the worst of the soreness in my Achilles, thanks to my easy pace over the flat road. Mentally, I was determined to keep pushing, telling myself, "I got this."

To keep that positive mindset and forward progress, my next goal was coffee. I made an abrupt right turn when I saw the Basecamp coffee shop. Inside, I took in the wonderful aroma of freshly brewed coffee. Ahhhh. Happy place.

While drinking coffee and eating blueberry muffins, I talked to an older couple who had done multi-day rides back in the '70s and '80s. They still loved the feel of the open road - now with motorcycles rather than bicycles. The woman made delicate prayer crosses and offered one to me for my journey. I felt bad declining her thoughtful gesture, but I knew it would end up breaking and I couldn't accept it.

Just when I was getting ready to head out, a guy stopped to talk to me about being out on the trail. He had backpacked the Continental Divide Trail (CDT) a few years earlier. Nothing lifts your spirits like meeting other people who have done adventures and receiving their well wishes to "enjoy the ride" and "good luck."

I was ready to get back on track. I pedaled through town looking for a grocery store to get a few food items and also address my rain gear situation. The thin patches of blue sky I had seen earlier in the morning were fading back to clouds, hinting at more rain to come. In an attempt to avoid wet, cold hands, I purchased blue dishwashing gloves at a grocery store. This was an experiment, after seeing other riders try the same back in Eureka. The Tour Divide was turning into a bunch of people riding around posing as dishwashers.

As I was packing up my bike, another racer rode into the parking lot and we started talking about the gloves. "Do you mind watching my bike while I go get a pair?" she asked.

"Sure. No problem."

While she was in the store, I packed up my food and found a place to store my new gloves.

As she returned with her new gloves, I said, "Hopefully these will keep our hands dry when it starts raining again."

"Thanks for watching my bike."

"You're welcome." I pointed to her singlespeed. "Nice bike. I'm on a Moots too."

"Thanks. It's been a great bike so far. I'm Alice, by the way."

"I'm Andy," I said as we shook hands.

With our food and gear packed away, we left town together and rode south on paved roads as the route carried us between the large Flathead Lake off to our right and the Swan Mountains in the distance to our left.

"We've been riding at about the same pace. I remember your green rain gear from when you arrived at the hotel in Eureka," I said.

"That was a brutal day. I was on the bike for twenty hours."

"These flat roads are a nice change of pace. How has the singlespeed been so far?" I asked.

"Well, I've never ridden anything but a singlespeed. So I guess it's good," Alice replied.

"You've never had a geared bike?"

"No. I started riding about six years ago and my first bike was a singlespeed. I've raced all over Oregon the past couple of years and I love having just one gear."

"That's awesome! Is this your first time on the Tour Divide?"

"Yes, This is my first multi-day race," she said.

"Same here. Great way to start with all of this bad weather," I said.

I rode at a casual pace and matched Alice's slower speed on flat pavement, limited by her single gear. I was more than happy to soft pedal, enjoying an easier section after the struggle to merely survive the previous three days. Over the next two hours, we continued to chat about our bikes, the weather, and our bikepacking gear.

"My setup was not ideal for this weather. I only have a mesh tent and my homemade rain pants aren't holding up."

"You made your rain gear?" I asked.

"Only the pants. I made them to match the jacket. The mesh sides are good for ventilation but they don't keep me dry."

"I don't think any of us have been dry since we started!"

The clouds hung low in the sky, taunting us. More rain was on the way.

We reached the café located at the Swan River crossroads and stopped for lunch. I checked the specials, and to my surprise it listed Biscuits and Gravy. Done. I do love me some biscuits and gravy. I think I could have ridden on biscuits and gravy, coffee, and ice cream for the entire ride. Too bad they don't carry well in a frame pack.

After lunch, the road led into the mountains, zigging and zagging a few times along the way. Underneath my tires, the pavement turned to gravel and the climbing began. Above, trees replaced the wide open views of the morning, and wrapped me like a cocoon. Within a few powerful pedal strokes, Alice zoomed ahead of me. Her climbing pace was unreal. I guess that's what always riding singlespeeds will do for you - make you super strong. My fourteen gears and I watched as she climbed further and further up the road until she vanished around a corner.

I began my solitary ascent up the first long climb of the day. Once I settled into a comfortable rhythm, I enjoyed climbing in the cool, overcast conditions and the quietness of the mountains. No cars. No cities. Only the sound of my breathing and the tires rolling over the dirt.

The clouds unleashed their rain as I crested the top of the climb. My rain jacket and rain pants made another appearance. It was only the fourth day, and I already hated rain pants. There is nothing comfortable about riding in them. But on a chilly, wet day with mud and rain, it was an unfortunate necessity.

Even in the mud and rain, the downhill was fun. I eventually caught back up to Alice after the downhill and some flatter sections where my gearing had an advantage. It was a pattern that would be repeated over and over again. I rode with Alice for almost five days, always amazed at her climbing pace. Within a few pedal strokes of starting a climb, it seemed like she was 100 yards ahead of me. Those climbing legs carried Alice to finish as the first place woman and 11th place overall, all while on a singlespeed.

With my hated rain pants, I kept plodding on through the mud and forest roads. Occasionally I would catch a glimpse of a pond or stream beside the road. One spot in particular really caught my eye. There was a stream running down the hill on the right side of the road. Surrounding the stream was every shade of green imaginable. Dark green trees, bright green moss on the rocks in the stream, ferns poking out from the shady spots, grasses up against the road. With all of the rain that had fallen, the stream was pouring down the hill and between the rocks. It was a scene that Bob Ross would have enjoyed with all of the happy trees and full use of the green color palette.

It seemed like the rain stopped each time I encountered an incline, whether a longer climb or just a small hill. As I crested the top, the rain started falling again. I guess that just made the downhills a little more "fun."

While riding on a flatter section through what looked like logging operations, I caught up to Alice, and we continued to ride through the trees and sporadic rain showers. Casey joined up with us as evening settled upon Montana. The three of us wound our way up, down, left, and right towards Holland Lake. The roads in this section were narrow with lots of trees. I can only imagine how beautiful this area would be in the daylight. As night approached, the rain started to fall much harder.

We all knew the Holland Lake Lodge was only a few miles down the road. Gritting of my teeth, I laid into the pedals a little harder to minimize my time out in these deteriorating conditions. The day started out dry and easy, but had turned dark, soaking wet, and getting worse with each pedal stroke.

A mile away from the lodge, the route crossed Highway 83. At the intersection I saw Klaus Thiel, a rider from Germany who kept roughly the same pace as me; we kept crossing paths at stores and in towns. He was also headed to the lodge.

Riding through the dark and the rain, Klaus, Alice, Casey and I all made it to Holland Lake Lodge. Other riders had arrived earlier in the night and were already asleep, preparing for an early morning departure. The lodge was way too upscale for stinky muddy riders, not your typical motel stop for the night. At that point, I wasn't about to go set up my tarp in the cold and rain. The price of the room included a full dinner with dessert, plus breakfast and lunch. Dinner was delicious and much better food than I was expecting to eat that night. While I would have rather been with my wife to enjoy the meal than with a bunch of dirty racers, it was nice to have good food and a warm bed for the night.

Since we were planning to leave before breakfast was served, the chef made us each two PB&J sandwiches to-go. I'm sure that's not a meal she made very often, but we were happy to have food that would travel well the following day.

Stephan, who I last saw when leaving Whitefish that morning, came into the lodge as we were finishing up our meals. As was his typical behavior, soon after he walked in the door there was gear strewn everywhere. Socks and jacket were hung up by the fire to dry. Food was on the overstuffed sofa. Shoes, helmet, and other cycling gear were scattered between the floor and various tables.

At one point he asked himself, "Where's my wallet?" in an exasperated voice.

We all replied in unison, "It's in your helmet on the table over there," pointing to the table in front of him.

We had been watching in awe as Stephan, the Tasmanian Devil, unpacked all of his gear, and we knew better than he did where everything had landed. We were still laughing as he picked up the wallet and paid for his room.

Casey and Stephan stayed in the lobby savoring a few beers. The rest of us were wiped out and headed upstairs to our respective rooms. Sleep did not come easily or in any great quantity that night. My brain was too wound up thinking about the next day. What did the route look like? What would the conditions be? Would the weather cooperate? What should be my final destination for the day? I would continue to ask myself these questions over the next few days.

I let my schedule dictate the day, instead of riding and seeing what each day brought. I wish I would have simply ridden and stopped when I was tired, rather than planning everything out in my head. It would have made for better sleep, as well as a better finish time, because my final stopping point for each day would not have been set in my mind at the start of the day. I fought this issue the entire ride - determining a final destination for each day in my head, and then not pushing past that point if I arrived early, or struggling to make it if the day took longer than planned.

With little sleep, the alarm went off at 5:30 a.m. Outside I could hear a steady rain, not an enjoyable sound when you know that you will start the day soaked. Well, I guess hearing a bear outside of your tent would be a worse way to wake up.

Several pictures of Holland Lake hung in the lobby. One stunningly beautiful picture featured a canoe in the water under a perfect blue sky surrounded by mountains. Unfortunately, thanks to the weather, I never saw Holland Lake, or the jagged beauty of the Canadian Rockies, or the vistas overlooking ever-green covered mountains in Montana during the first week of the race. Besides riding in the race, I looked forward to experiencing natural beauty of areas I had never visited before. I would have to take in those scenes on another trip.

On this morning, the clouds hung low, and the rain was coming down harder than it had the previous day. The good news was that all of my gear was dry and warm when I got dressed. Of course, my feet ended up soaked within the first few minutes of riding through the deluge and standing water on the road.

Alice and I packed our PB&J sandwiches and opted for a breakfast of sugary junk food. We pedaled away from the warmth and comfort of the lodge into the darkness and the rain. From Holland Lake Lodge, the Tour Divide route takes you immediately onto the infamous climb up Richmond Peak.

It's not the actual riding that makes Richmond Peak one of the well-known climbs of the Tour Divide. Instead, it's the section featuring the 45 degree off-camber side slope that riders traverse, typically while walking over the ground still covered with the previous winter's snow. One misstep could send a rider tumbling down the mountain, with only a tree or a rock to break the fall on a slope that steep. There is also the challenge of staying on track when walking on top of snow and unable to see the actual route.

My wheels rolled through the stream of water that flowed down the road. Between the water spray coming up from the road and the heavy rain falling from the sky, everything was soaked. Somehow, I managed to settle into a comfortable climbing rhythm while Alice powered away from me.

The rain stopped about halfway up the climb. Good news, right? Not when the rain stops and the snowfall begins. A forest service truck passed me as I was riding in the fresh falling snow. They looked so toasty and warm inside the truck, probably with a hot coffee thermos in the seat between them. I kept climbing, and the snow kept falling. Several inches of fresh snow had fallen. Then the route turned left and I encountered the existing snow that had not yet melted off of the mountain. The combination of last winter's snow and the day's fresh snow were my companions on Richmond Peak.

The snow was so heavy, it had covered not just the trail but also all of the pine trees lining the route. It was a winter wonderland in the middle of June. The only way to move forward was to walk and push the bike; riding was not an option. Pushing a bike through all this snow while unable to see the trail makes for very slow going. The words "this is stupid" kept running through my mind.

I was beginning to get really cold. Those blue gloves from the grocery store in Columbia Falls weren't doing much now to keep me warm. My time as a happy dishwasher was over. I had three layers of gloves on and all of them were soaked. My fingers were going numb. The process of walking for a bit and then checking my GPS to make sure I was still on the route was not generating enough body heat to keep me warm.

After what felt like hours, I made it to the steep side slope that I had read about from other riders. It's billed as a 45 degree angle with snow, downed trees and nothing to really stop you if you fall. Unfortunately for me, those accounts were completely accurate. There really is a steep drop off to the left. With the clouds and snow, I couldn't see the bottom down below. I tried my best not to find out how far down it went.

Pushing my bike through this section was quite a challenge. With each step, I tried to find the imprints of the riders that had gone through earlier. That was better than trying to make fresh tracks in unknown snow. Making these steps with cycling shoes is not easy. Several times, my foot slipped and I slid down a couple of feet until either snow or a branch caught me. Not good. This was not a day for sledding down the mountain.

The snow kept falling. I kept trudging along at a very slow pace. My hands and feet were now completely numb. I started to shiver and worry crept into my mind. I could see on my GPS that I was close to the top of the climb. Close doesn't mean much when you are pushing at one or two miles per hour. In the interest of warmth and safety, I pulled out my down jacket to wear under my rain jacket. The rain jacket had soaked through, which meant the down was going to get wet and not insulate nearly as well. At that moment, I only cared about being warmer, even if it meant the down jacket would not be much use the rest of the day.

The only clothing left in my seat bag were my sleep clothes - a wool t-shirt and wool boxers. *Do I put those on as well or save them to wear whenever I get to somewhere that's dry? If I do put them on, that means taking off all of my rain gear and exposing myself to more cold, and I'm so cold already.* I decided to leave those clothes in my seat bag so I would have something dry to wear later.

Worst case, I set up my tarp, change into my dry clothes, and hope my sleeping quilt would keep me warm. I had a plan for the cold. I still had to get through the climb.

My progress went something like this:

1. Push bike up steep incline.
2. Step forward to catch up to the bike.
3. Push bike.
4. Step forward.
5. Fall into hip-deep hole created by a fallen tree and hidden by the layers of snow.
6. Bike lands on top of me.
7. Remove the fifty-pound bike while stuck in hole.
8. Climb out of hole.
9. Repeat.

This happened multiple times as my steps managed to punch through the deep snow. Arrgh! Frustration started to get the better of me. Luckily, I managed to crest the top of the hill and start the process of walking back down. The downhill wasn't much easier physically because there was so much snow on the ground. But mentally, I knew I was on the downhill and the snow had to stop at some point.

It had been at least five hours since leaving Holland Lake, and I had managed barely more than twenty miles. On a typical day of bikepacking, I would have travelled fifty miles in that same time period.

Although my climbing pace could not match Alice's, my walking-in-snow pace was faster. I caught back up to her just before the snow pack ended. At that elevation, the snow had stopped falling, replaced with a misty rain. We were both frozen and shivering. The good news was a long downhill was the only thing between us and Seeley Lake where we could get food and warm up.

Decision time. *Do I fly down the hill and get to town faster but colder? Or do I go slower and stay out in the cold a bit longer?* I chose to fly down the hill in order to arrive in Seeley Lake faster. Smart decision? I don't know if anything was smart at that point. The only solution was getting to some shelter where my clothes could dry out and core temperatures could rise.

The downhill felt a lot like the first downhill I experienced in the Triple Bypass back in Colorado. My body was shivering so much, I could feel it pushing the bike from side to side. All I could do was keep going. I had no more clothing or rain gear left to shield me from the elements.

With my hands frozen to the handlebar and feet that felt like blocks of ice, I managed to ride into the town of Seeley Lake. My eyes scanned the buildings and signs for the first resemblance of a restaurant or store. A hotel on my left caught my eye, but I wasn't quite ready to give up just yet. First, I wanted to get some food and stand inside a building with heat.

We found a restaurant and walked in shivering, dripping water, and looking miserable. The restaurant didn't care and they were happy to have us as customers. I sat in a booth, shivering as I drank coffee and ate soup. As long as I stayed still I felt warm-ish. Any movement brought shivers. The hot liquids eventually warmed me from the inside and seemed to stop the shivering. My meal of a burger and fries still did not get me to the point of feeling warm. I knew I had to go outside and keep riding. However, as soon as I stepped outside, I started to shiver again.

"Alice, I can't do this. I'm already shivering again," I said as I put my leg over the top tube. A mere thirty miles into the day and I was seriously considering staying in Seeley Lake for the night.

"Well..." she paused for a moment. "We've only been thirty miles today."

"I know, I know. But I can't go back out there like this."

"Do you want to go back into the restaurant? Or maybe we should go to the bike shop across the street?" as she pointed at the sign.

"Yeah, that's a good idea. They might have a new rain jacket since this one is soaked through."

We crossed the street to the Rocky Mountain Adventure Gear bike shop. Mike and Cathy, the owners, were like so many other people I ran into on the Divide. Overly nice and extremely happy to take great care of all of the riders that came through. In the shop, I found a new rain jacket and winter gloves to help me take on the frigid day. Alice also purchased a pair of winter gloves that Cathy had been holding for herself. Knowing that Alice needed the gloves more at that moment, she selflessly allowed Alice to purchase them.

Armed with my new gear, I still wasn't ready to ride out in the cold rain that continued to fall outside. While the shivering had stopped, I could tell that my core temperature was still low.

Mike brought out a space heater, made me sit in front of it, and wrapped me in blankets to warm me up. Oh, that heat felt so good. It was even better than biscuits and gravy. Of course, everyone was laughing at me and taking pictures of the poor guy wrapped up in blankets. I didn't care. I was smiling through all of it.

10

Stubborn

FIVE DAYS IN AND THE Tour Divide was kicking my butt left, right, up, and down. There isn't any other way to put it. The weather was relentless in it's nastiness. During my training for the race, I had ridden in worse conditions, however, the onslaught of bad weather day after day compounded to make the first five days of the race the worst conditions I had ever encountered while riding a bike.

The horrible weather and sore Achilles were not going to make me stop. I wasn't giving in. Not then, not ever. My stubbornness was not going to be defeated that easily. If anything helped me out during the start of the race, it was my stubborn streak, one that has always been quite wide. It kept me pushing myself to my limits.

Sitting there in Seeley Lake wrapped in blankets, my stubbornness was taking a really good thrashing. Quitting wasn't an option, but stopping for the day was a serious consideration. The Tour Divide is as much a mental race as it is a physical race. Or in Yogi Berra terms - The Tour Divide is "ninety percent mental, the other half is physical." Stubbornness can make up for some of the physical and mental parts of the ride. On the fifth day of the race, this was certainly the case; my stubbornness combined with encouragement from Alice kept me moving forward, even though the logical part of my brain was telling me to stop.

In the back of my head, I knew I only had one chance at finishing this race. My wife jokingly kept mentioning this as the start of the race neared; however, we both knew it to be quite true. The race simply took too much planning, training, and time away from my family for me to race it a second time. Eminem's song *Lose Yourself* kept repeating in my mind as I thought about the one shot I had at the race.

I knew I had to seize the opportunity. I couldn't let it slip. Stopping was not an option.

Why would someone choose to subject themselves to the pain and suffering required to ride unsupported for 2700 miles? Why ride through horrible weather day after day for five days, especially when you're not at the front, not even within several days of the leaders, out of contention for the win? Most of us do this race for personal reasons. As fellow racer Sarah Caylor mentioned to me during the race, we were on a "vision quest", discovering ourselves during the journey. We were the mid-pack racers realizing how our limits, both physical and mental, could be broken when we pushed harder than we previously thought. It's amazing what can happen when we are forced to dig deeper than ever before.

The "vision quest" analogy was very fitting for my reasons to race. I also had another reason. I wanted to show my two boys, ages seven and nine at the time, that through hard work and determination we can make our dreams a reality. My dream of riding the Tour Divide began five years earlier after reading

"The Way of the Mountain Turtle" by Kent Petersen in an issue of *Dirt Rag*. Planning, buying gear, riding more than ever before, more planning, more riding - it was all part of my dream. All of the hard work was worth it to see the dream become reality. It's something I wanted them to understand. Nothing worthwhile ever comes easy.

Regardless of the reasons, a steady dose of a stubborn attitude helps push riders through the tough sections and low points that inevitably occur on a race of this length. Others may call it grit, "never give in," perseverance, drive, or determination. Whatever you call it, you must be willing to endure pain and discomfort to surpass prior limits and reach a goal.

Since I was a young kid, I've had a streak of stubbornness a mile wide, causing lots of frustration for my parents. My mom loves to tell the story of my attitude and my coloring books. I was four years old, and for some reason I was acting up. (It must have been my mom's fault because I was always a perfect kid, stubbornness and all.) I was misbehaving, so she had to resorted to punishment. Back in those days, punishment didn't come in the form of timeouts, it came in the form of a good ol' fashioned spanking. Nothing too severe, but enough to make a kid understand they did something wrong.

Except that my mom's spankings didn't have the intended result. Instead of me learning my lesson after the first spanking, I replied to her with, "That didn't hurt," and I'm sure some sort of smarty pants look on my face. The second spanking was a bit harder but had the same result - me declaring "That didn't hurt" even louder. Finally, after another spanking with the same response, my mom changed tactics.

She found my coloring books and crayons on the floor. She ripped a page from the book. The look on my face changed. My mom knew she had found a trigger point. "I don't care," was my response this time. Out came another page. "I don't care." Then a crayon was broken in two. "I don't care." When the second crayon was broken, so was I. It took several spankings, coloring book pages, and crayons before my mom prevailed. I guess every stubborn side has a breaking point. (Note to Mom: thanks for destroying my career as an artist. You can stop smiling now. I know you won that battle and many more while I was growing up.)

If I'm the kid with the coloring book, the climb up Richmond Peak had been the spankings, the heavy snow falling was the coloring book pages, and the shivering downhill to Seeley Lake was the first crayon being broken in two. If a couple more crayons had been broken that day, my stubborn streak might have cracked.

Fortunately, stubbornness and determination held out just a little bit longer. It would have been very easy to call it a day in Seeley Lake after only thirty miles, devising a plan to leave at 3:00 a.m. the next morning to get back on track. My stubbornness had other plans. I had a goal that morning when I left Holland Lake Lodge, and I didn't want to stop this far away from it. It proved to be one of the best uses of my stubborn streak during the race

11

Midnight Stargazing

IN THE COMFY, WARM CONFINES of the bike shop, the rain finally let up. I took off the blankets. I felt alive again.

Alice and I packed up our gear and headed out for the two mile climb from Seeley Lake back to the Tour Divide route. As we pedaled towards Ovando, Montana and their famed hospitality, the temperature remained in the low 40's. Outfitted in my new rain jacket and winter gloves, I barely managed to stay warm.

The dirt road meandered alongside a river. The clouds hung low in the sky, which meant I was missing yet another amazing stretch of scenery. One of the things I looked forward to most was the chance to ride in this beautiful country, but the weather wasn't allowing me to see the scenery of Canada and Montana. I could only imagine how great the mountains, pine trees, river, and a blue sky above it all would combine into a stunning landscape.

Ovando is a small, tiny town in western Montana. It sits halfway between Missoula to the west and Helena to the east. The town has a population of fifty and consists of three roads - Main Street, Pine Street, and Birch Street. Yes, it's a tiny town.

And it's also a special town to Tour Divide riders. They welcome every rider into town and offer riders a unique opportunity to stay in their jail, covered wagon, or tipi overnight.

Cresting the hill into Ovando, I heard, "Hey, Andy Amick, you've got a message!" Angler, as she's known on the bikepacking.net forums, had written down messages for riders and posted them on a bulletin board. How awesome is that!

My message read, "Your wife and kids are watching your progress closely. Grateful to everybody. Keep it going!" It was a huge boost to read the message from my family. Tears rolled out of my eyes as I kept reading the message over and over. The cold and pain of the day dissipated. Pushing on to Ovando had been the right decision.

At the Stray Bullet Café the food was good, but the people were better. They were getting ready to close when Alice and I rolled into Ovando. We were told to get in there fast and get some food. Every menu item had a gun or western name which made sense given that it was the "Stray Bullet Cafe." Although, this little tidbit took a while to register with my cold, snow, and water-logged brain.

The woman running the cafe was an absolute hoot! I could see her being the life of the party everywhere she went. She was funny, very matter of fact, and kept refilling the Coke in my glass. Her sports were hunting and fishing, not cycling. She liked to make jokes about our cycling situation - sore butts, silly for not having an engine, etc. It was all in good fun and it made for some good laughs. Maybe the first real laughs of the ride for me.

In all of my Tour Divide planning, I kept trying to make a schedule work out so I could stay the night in Ovando. Unfortunately, I came through in the late afternoon, and wanted to continue on over Huckleberry Pass and to the town of Lincoln.

It was a short stay in Ovando, but it was the most awesome town along the route. The message they posted from my wife, the welcome as I entered town, and the weather finally breaking for the first time in the race combined to make it a very memorable stop.

Back on the road my thoughts kept going back to the movie *Tombstone* where Val Kilmer as Doc Holliday says, "I'm your Huckleberry." It's a line I say to my wife quite often as a joke. Only this time, there was no laughing as the mountains loomed larger with each pedal stroke along the long flat stretch of ranch roads between Ovando and Huckleberry Pass. Coming into the right hand switchback that signaled the start of the climb, I changed into an easier gear.

Instead of an agonizing slow grind to the top, I found my favorite climb of the entire Tour Divide. The bright sunlight filtered through the trees as I wound my way up Huckleberry Pass in an almost euphoric state. Each rotation of the pedals felt easier than the last. My eyes gazed out upon the flat farmland below. My smile grew wider and wider.

Alice climbed faster than me, like she always did, and caught me about halfway up the mountain. But then something unusual happened. Feeling the boost from the sunshine, I kept up with her as we rode together for the remainder of the climb. It was the only time I ever matched her climbing pace.

I'll always remember climbing up Huckleberry as the sun set, and then flying down the pass in the dark to Lincoln. This is why we ride the Tour Divide. In the span of a few hours, you can go from the brink of exhaustion in the worst possible conditions to an explosion of sunshine, amazing people, and breathtaking scenery.

In Lincoln, Alice and I checked into the first hotel we found. The day started before dawn in a pouring rain, and finished at 11:00 p.m. with gear strewn about the room to dry. Although it was 100 of the toughest miles I had ever encountered, I made it through the day. I got this.

Before falling asleep, Alice asked me, "Does everything hurt when you lay down?"

"Oh yeah, and it's really bad when I turn over onto my shoulder."

"These long days are really taking a toll," she said.

Like the first days after starting a new workout routine, every muscle was sore to the touch. Just the movement of laying down in a bed was painful.

In spite of the aches and pains, I slept well that night. The next morning, the sky held the hope and promise of a dry day. Even though it was still cloudy and quite chilly, I could feel the tide starting to change.

Lincoln was one of those towns that a Tour Divide racer enjoys simply because all of the amenities - restaurant, hotel, bar, and gas station - were on one street. It was an easy town. Easy to find the hotel at night. Easy to find food and coffee the following morning.

Less than seven hours after arriving in Lincoln, Alice and I rode out of town in the cool, calm morning air. The houses on the outskirts of town gave way to small farms and then to large ranches before the road headed up the long climb of Stemple Pass.

The climb had several pitches that were rideable if one was willing to expend a lot of energy to go about the same pace as walking. I chose walking, something several past riders have written about. There is no need to push too hard this early in the race, a lesson that was reinforced after my over-exertion on the second day. With a fully loaded bike, I had given up on trying to ride anything that caused me to shift into my lowest two gears. It was far easier to walk and catch my breath.

At the top, I watched a young rider float his way up the steep pitch like it was a flat road. I later found out that the rider was Calvin Decker, who ended up finishing in second place overall. Calvin started the race slow, gradually increasing his pace until finally there was only one rider ahead of him.

The downhill from Stemple Pass was simply fantastic - straight, fast, and steep. A few times, I caught myself going too fast for the conditions, especially with a loaded bike and 2000 miles left in the race. Calvin came flying past me with a happy grin yelling, "This is great!" And that, folks, is the full extent of the conversation I had with a Tour Divide podium finisher.

After another grinding climb and downhill, I caught up to Alice, who had been stopped by a train. Literally stopped by a train that was sitting on the tracks. We talked for a bit about the train and then we heard someone on the other side of the train. It turned out to be Lindsay Shepherd who was a northbound racer.

"Hey there! I thought I heard someone else," Lindsay said as we looked at each other through a gap in the train cars.

"This in interesting. Didn't expect a train to slow me down today. Have you been here long?" I asked.

"No, just got here."

The front of the train was a ways up the track, but there was a flatbed car a few feet away from where the road crossed the tracks. We decided that climbing over the flatbed was our best option. Lifting a loaded bike up onto a train car is not the easiest thing to do. Alice and I climbed up and over first. When we got to the other side, we talked to Lindsay a bit more before she said goodbye to us and carried her bike over the flatbed.

Helena was less than twenty miles from the train with only a mellow climb up Priest Pass in between. Just outside of town, Alice and I passed by a house with Tour Divide signs and bags placed on a table. After we had passed the house, we both decided it was worth a second look so we turned around.

Score! There were bags that contained a combination of trail mix, Swedish Fish, and dried mangoes. Oh, dried mangoes are really tasty. With a bag of goodies, we rode into town and decided to call it a day at 3:00 p.m. after only sixty-five miles. The forecast called for more rain later that afternoon. I was happy to avoid more rain while taking advantage of some downtime to ice my knee and Achilles.

That night, dry and warm in a comfy bed, I only slept for a few hours before I woke at 2:00 a.m., unable to go back to sleep. My crazy mind was spinning and thinking and doing everything except sleep.

Rolling out of town the next morning was a struggle. The coffee shops and gas stations I passed were closed. Caffeine was a no-go. My sore left knee felt much worse than the day before. The route from Helena to Butte and over Fleecer Ridge, my goal for the day, contained over 12,000 feet of climbing. How can one climb with a very sore knee and without coffee?

I found out very quickly. The city of Helena seemed to vanish shortly after the downtown section. At one point there were a few houses, and then a few feet later there was nothing. The road turned to dirt and headed into the mountains.

Already, Alice had pulled out ahead of me, getting further with each of her powerful pedal strokes. While we technically "rode" together for five days, we rarely rode side-by-side during a day. On the first day leaving Columbia Falls we kept the same pace on the flat paved roads. Since that time, there had been very few flat spots. On the climbs, I rode alone with Alice somewhere up the road. On the downhills, I was usually alone again trying to make up the time that I lost on the climb. Occasionally, I would catch her at the top as she stopped to put on extra layers or eat a snack. And often, at the bottom of a climb when it flattened out, my gearing allowed me to catch back up. The vast majority of the time, we were each riding our own pace as a solo rider.

After about an hour of climbing, it was time for drastic measures. I pulled over on the side of the road and dumped a few packets of "emergency" instant coffee into my Platypus bottle, trying to make something that resembled coffee. Turns out, cold, bitter, instant coffee is only one notch above no coffee.

I climbed at a steadier pace as the caffeine gave me a spark and my knee loosened up. On the downhill off of the unnamed climb, I caught up to Alice.

Up next was a tight, steep, technical climb up Lava Mountain. Towards the top, mud, rocks, and roots managed to reduce the climb to one of mostly walking. While I navigated over drops, around tight turns and under branches on the ensuing downhill, one of those branches decided to jump out and grab my jacket. It ripped a hole in the right shoulder of my brand new Seeley Lake jacket.

"Stupid freakin' trees!" I yelled out as I kept riding through the tight trails.

"Are you ok?" Alice asked.

"Yeah, just pissed that I tore my new jacket. That was a lot of money that I just ripped." My frustration stemmed from feeling like I just wasted my money. But the jacket got me out of Seeley Lake, so even torn it was money well spent.

The downhill flattened out into a wide open treeless approach to the town of Basin. After a short lunch break at the one restaurant in town, Alice and I rode towards Butte on a frontage road that deteriorated into what the map called a "non-maintained cattle access trail" (basically a two track path) as it paralleled the Boulder River for several miles.

Along this stretch, Alice and I ran into a herd of cattle. There are more cattle than anything else on the Divide. Most of the time, you can ride towards the cattle, make some noise, and they will disperse. Every once in a while, one would stand on the side of the road and stare you down. When this occurred, I rode past them, hoping they would remain still. However, passing by a large bull while it stares directly at you is unsettling.

On this day, we had a cow that couldn't figure out how to get off of the road. The cow would run off the side of the road only to come back onto the road a few hundred yards later. This happened over and over. The poor animal must have been so tired. Just when we thought it had figured out how to stay off of the road, it would run back into our path. We were laughing so hard, we could barely ride. Eventually, the cow stopped running and stood in the grass to the side of the road so we could pass.

After crossing under the interstate, the route meandered through smaller hills, past the Mormon Gulch Campground, and topped out on a hill overlooking the town of Butte. From our vista, we saw the city below us and the Berkeley Pit, a defunct open pit copper mine, to our left.

Butte is the biggest town along the Tour Divide, and is also home to the Outdoorsman bike shop, one of the famous stops on the route. They are known for taking great care of the riders and their bikes, which are usually in need of some maintenance and replacement parts after almost 800 miles of racing.

Even with all of the rain, mud, and snow, I only needed to clean my chain and replace my front brake pads to keep me going. I was lucky my bike held up so well in the conditions that caused major mechanical issues for other riders. My good fortune was due to Nic, who meticulously built each component of my bike in preparation for the race.

It was late afternoon when we left Butte. Our goal? To finish at Wise River that evening, completing 130 miles and 12,000 feet of climbing for the day.

But first, we had to conquer Fleecer Ridge. Unlike most mountains on the Tour Divide, this one is famous for the downhill rather than the climbing. At the top, the ridge looks like it drops off of a ledge, into an extremely steep and rocky trail. For many, it's deemed unrideable.

Unfortunately, I read the map wrong and thought the ridge was only fifteen miles from Butte. Turns out, it was actually thirty miles with another large climb over the Continental Divide between Butte and Fleecer Ridge. Oops! A long day of climbing got a little bit harder.

The extra climb started on pavement, which turned to dirt as it steadily rose. I reached the top as the sun was starting to set. My reward was a glorious view with the last rays of sunshine highlighting the hills. Sprinkles of golden hues highlighted peaks as far as I could see. Above, soft clouds floated in the blue sky. In front of me, the road dropped off of the backside of the mountain.

After soaking in the view and taking plenty of pictures, I enjoyed one helluva screaming downhill - 1500 feet of vertical drop with a sweeping road that required very little in the way of brakes.

The sun sank behind the mountains as we crossed under the interstate for the third time that day. We began climbing towards Fleecer Ridge.

While stopping to refill my water at one of the many campgrounds along the road, I noticed a campfire coming from the only site occupied in the campground. The man sitting by the fire invited us over to chat and enjoy the warmth of the fire. It was a welcomed break from the climbing and the cool night temperatures.

A few minutes into our conversation, he asked "Do you carry a gun?"

"No, just bear spray," I said.

"Well, I always carry my gun with me out here. See, it will protect me from the bears," he said as he pulled out the gun and showed us.

When you see a guy all alone in a deserted campground with a gun by his side, it makes you a little nervous.

Luckily, he changed the subject and asked us how we could keep riding day after day. He said that he hoped his kids could one day take on an adventure like the one we were living out. These brief conversations with strangers were some of the best parts of the ride. Meeting people who don't ride bikes, sharing stories, and making a small connection with them makes you feel a little less alone as you ride towards Mexico.

We rode away from the comfortable fire to finish the climb. The final 1000 vertical feet of climbing started to hurt. It had been a very long day. A deep darkness surrounded us - the kind that occurs when there is only a sliver of moon and you are far away from towns. We neared the top as the clock approached midnight.

The road turned left onto a two-track trail with a waist deep gully in between the tracks. It was too steep for riding, which was just as well because it was almost impossible to find the path. I kept a close eye on my GPS track as I pushed to the top.

Fleecer Ridge opened up into an exposed meadow with no trees. Complete darkness surrounded me. Above, the sky was awash in stars. Atop the ridge, I took in the grandeur of the night. Total calm. Total silence. Total awe. At a moment like that, you realize just how very tiny you are in the world and the universe.

If it wasn't for the cold that quickly settled in, I would have stayed there much longer, taking in the night. But the cold and the promise of a super-steep downhill called me on. As a personal challenge, I wanted to tame this "unrideable" trail.

It took several attempts to locate the trail. Once found, it was steep and rocky, but definitely rideable. In the darkness, all I could see was the trail a few feet in front of me. At first, I couldn't tell if it was getting steeper. It did! Now the stories were making more sense. It was really, really steep with a lot of loose rocks. Still determined to ride, I made it about one-third of the way down before I decided to walk down since it was so dark. Walking is a relative term. I gripped both brake levers tightly and took big steps through the loose rock, sliding down the trail to prevent myself from tumbling head over heels.

It turns out, all of the stories people tell about Fleecer Ridge are true.

12

Technical Riding

OVERALL, THE TOUR DIVIDE DOES not require much in the way of technical mountain biking skills. There are a handful of sections that are singletrack or technical. Fleecer is the most infamous due to stories of riders attempting the downhill only to crash and tumble down the steep trail.

Why did I choose to ride down this very steep trail on a clear cold night after having ridden over 130 tough miles that day? I wanted to. I *had* to. Simple as that. In my mind, prior to the start of the Tour Divide, I told myself that I needed to ride Fleecer. It was a technical challenge, especially with a fully loaded bike. Not to mention it was dark, cold, and the end of a long day.

Since my first days of mountain biking, finding rocky, rooted trails with steep drops and twisty turns in the trees has always been fun. I guess that's why I enjoy mountain biking so much. Growing up in South Carolina, there were plenty of places to practice riding in mud and over roots to hone my technical skills. One place in particular was the Spiderwoman trail at

Harbison State Forest. Whenever Stan and I rode at Harbison, we always included at least one attempt of Spiderwoman.

The trail was very short, consisting of a steep, rocky and root filled ravine. Gravity made getting to the bottom easy, as long as a rider avoided the biggest of the rocks. A few twists and turns to the bottom and then it was a very steep grind to the top. The steepness required a slow climbing speed to maintain traction. The slow speed also meant that each rock, twist, or root was easily able to throw me off course or stop my momentum. Failure was the accepted norm. On a really good day of bike handling, perfect weight balance, and a little bit of luck, I could fight my way to the top without putting a foot down. It didn't happen very often. When it did, I had truly earned it, just like they always said in those EF Hutton commercials from the 1980's.

Spiderwoman and the trails at Harbison prepared me for my first mountain bike race at the 1995 Cactus Cup in Atlanta. If memory serves, the course was not overly technical and there was not much elevation change. A few creek crossings were thrown in for some interesting obstacles. Easy enough.

There was, however, one stubborn tree to deal with. One tree. One big tree all by itself to the side of the trail. On our practice lap the day before the race, the tree attacked me. I was just riding along, getting a feel for the trail. Next thing I know, I'm off the trail and heading straight towards the one tree that's not even close to the course. Mesmerized by what was happening, I could not make my body steer the bike left or right. I ran smack dab into the tree. The only noise was the crunch of my brake lever hitting the tree and me saying "uuugggghhhh" as I came to an abrupt stop. The bike stayed upright. I stayed on the bike. I can still hear Stan laughing at me. One lonely tree, several feet off of the trail, managed to get me. So much for my technical riding abilities.

Based on my training lap, I made sure not to hit that tree during the race. I succeeded in my goal and managed to finish the race tree-free.

Technical riding on the East Coast is very different from technical riding in the Rockies, which has more rocks, open trails, loose dirt, and faster speeds. The White Ranch and Walker Ranch trails outside of Boulder, Colorado became my go-to trails, and I did my best to keep up with my roommate Tony, who was a much better technical and downhill rider than me. I figured if he could go that fast, I could increase my own speed and not have him leave me so far behind.

While trying to ride faster downhills, I got a lot of experience with crashing and bent rims. "Taco-ing" at least one rim a month was a tough hit to a college student's budget. Financially, this forced me to get much better at identifying lines and staying upright, keeping my rims rideable. By the end of that first year in Colorado, my skills had improved, and more importantly my understanding of how to ride had improved enough to stop the cash outflows for new rims.

In those first two years of my Colorado living, I managed to ride in many different places including Moab, Utah; Boulder, Colorado; and Golden Gate State Park outside of Golden, Colorado. Outside of training for and racing the Tour Divide, it was the best period of my biking "career." Riding almost every day, finding new trails, picking up new technical skills, getting better and faster on the downhills, and meeting new cycling friends made for some great times.

Those years of testing my technical limits on the tight, root-filled, muddy Southeast trails and the rocky, open, fast Western trails gave me the confidence to ride down Fleecer Ridge. I still had an anxious moment as the bike first rolled over the edge and began quickly descending the steep and loose trail. Visions of crashing and rolling down the hill floated in my head. Despite the nerves, my hands remained steady on the handlebars and my headlight kept me focused on my line. Challenge completed.

13

Alone

FLEECER RIDGE PROVED TO BE every bit as difficult as riders reported, forcing me to walk down part of the steep incline. With the steepest section of the ridge conquered, I remounted my bike and continued riding.

Getting down Fleecer Ridge in the darkness was quite an experience. Not only was it the last obstacle in an epic day of riding, but it also became one of those rare special moments in my bike riding life. At the top of the ridge, I gazed at the night sky admiring the vastness of the world and the aloneness that its size can bring. By the time I reached the bottom, I knew the world, the bike, and the rider had aligned, just as they had in North Carolina many years prior when a bird flew within the beam of my headlight, to move at the same rhythm as my pedaling.

After crossing the river at the bottom of the ridge, the terrain flattened out into a slight downhill. There was at least another hour of riding to make it to the next town, Wise River. The combination of the clear night skies and riding alongside a creek caused the temperature to plunge. Once again, I pulled out my rain jacket and donned my winter gloves.

Eventually, houses came into view and the dirt road turned to pavement. It was a few more miles until Wise River, which turned out to be nothing more than a few buildings, all of them closed for the night. Working with the limited information on the map, I never knew what I was going to get from one town to the next. I guess it's a bit like Forrest Gump and his chocolates.

"I guess this is the campground that the map listed," I said to Alice, as we found a few sites in the grass behind the café.

"Yeah, it's not much. Should we stay here?"

Looking around, we saw one other tent set up. There was nothing "official" about the sites, and nowhere to leave money. We figured the morning would have us up and riding before anything was open.

"My bivy would fit under this picnic table. Your tent would be ok in the grass."

"I don't know. I'm not comfortable just sleeping here without paying. Maybe we should ride down the road to see if we can find somewhere else." Alice responded.

It was late, we were tired, yet here we were debating a proper spot to camp. A week later in the race, I would have setup under the picnic table or even on the front porch of the café, like other riders have done in the past. But at this point, I was still learning the ropes of being a Tour Divide rider.

Instead of staying at the "campground," we headed up the road and found a place to camp on the side of the road. Turns out, that was a big mistake! We ended up in a low lying area filled with tall grass. What happens when you have a low lying area with tall grass on a moist evening? Yep, everything was covered in dew that soaked through my bivy and sleeping bag. It was a miserable night compounded by the fact that I didn't get much sleep for a second night in a row. It was the kind of night where I lay restless, the same thoughts circling in my head. When I woke, I wasn't sure if I had slept at all.

There was no way I could continue with nights like the one in Wise River or Helena. I wasn't even out of Montana yet. Lack of sleep was starting to wreak havoc on my mind and body.

In the morning, I packed up my gear in a groggy haze. My craving for coffee, breakfast, and more coffee was put on hold because the café in Wise River didn't open until later in the morning. I made several trips from the campsite on the side of the road to Wise River, one to check on breakfast, one to check another building that looked like a restaurant, and one for a bathroom break. If someone had been watching my SPOT tracker that morning, they would have thought I was crazy or lost. Maybe even both. With little to no sleep and zero coffee, my day was off to a rough start.

I left Wise River after eating a candy bar and some other gas station food purchased in Butte the day before. The day's ride began on a paved National Scenic Byway that paralleled the Wise River, until it climbed 2000 feet over an unnamed pass. From there, a long downhill led to food options in Polaris. I was less than forty miles away from food and caffeine.

No problem. It's paved and should be easy.

The phrase "should be easy" is one that should never, ever get into the mind of a Tour Divide rider. Easy sections do not exist. Just when you think one is coming up, the weather, your body, or fatigue will reach out and bring you back to the cold reality of how hard the ride can be.

As I began my eighth day of riding, fatigue reached up from the depths with it's cold, scraggly fingers and pulled me into an abyss where each pedal stroke became a struggle, even on paved roads.

I started out feeling good with a sugar high from the candy bar breakfast, and was actually riding ahead of Alice. When the road pitched up, she soon caught and dropped me. A few minutes later, I was left walking up a paved road barely making forward progress.

I completely lacked energy. For some reason, I never considered taking the caffeine pills stored in the front pouch of my handlebar bag. I added the pills to my kit thinking that I would use them on the long days of riding into the night. The idea of using them during the mornings when there was no coffee available never crossed my mind. In hindsight, taking a couple of them probably would have made the morning a little more bearable and the road a little more rideable for this coffee-addict.

Instead, I found myself walking up a paved road, which does not put a cyclist into a good mindset. After what felt like hours, the top of the climb finally came into view. And what a view it was. The trees lining the road opened into a high mountain meadow with lush green grass, framed by mountains with a fresh coat of snow on their peaks.

The clouds over the mountains began to drop a cold misty rain. I put on my rain jacket and pedaled on to begin the long awaited downhill to Polaris. As is the case with many downhills, this one contained a few uphill sections that caused me to walk again. I felt awful. No energy, no motivation.

So much for the easy stretch of pavement.

As I came around a sweeping corner I saw the turnoff to the Elkhorn Hot Springs resort, a steep uphill climb. Food was there, within a few minutes of walking up the hill. But I couldn't endure any more walking that morning. Without even a second thought, I continued down the road towards Polaris.

Tucked into my aero bars with the misty rain dissipating, the swooping fast downhill raised my spirits. Once down into the valley, I saw houses and a sign for Ma Barnes' Country Store. I had found my source for the food and refreshment I so badly needed. I knew I had to stop, recharge, get some caffeine, and sit down on something that wasn't a bicycle seat.

When I rolled up to the store, Sarah Caylor and Alice were enjoying their lunch of snacks, pizzas, and sodas. After fueling up with a few snacks, I still felt like a shell of myself. Alice and Sarah took off and I sat there eating and thinking. While I certainly did not want to ride at that moment, I also knew I didn't what to quit the race either.

I bought more drinks, snacks, and bananas (whenever fruit was available, it always tasted so good). I called into MTBCast, and then called my wife. I barely managed a few words without crying. I was a bumbling mess sitting on the picnic table outside of the store. Her words of encouragement began to bring me out of the depths of despair. When I talked to my kids, they kept saying, "Dad, you got this." I packed up and got my emotional and tired self back on the bike with the helpful push from my family.

For the first time in the entire ride, I was completely alone. Alice and Sarah were up the road about an hour. I had no idea who was behind me or how far back they were.

Before I made the right turn off of the pavement onto Bannack Road, I caught up to a woman riding the TransAmerica route. We had a brief chat while cruising along the pavement. When the road pitched up, I got ahead of her and then made the right turn onto dirt. "At least I'm riding faster than a touring road cyclist," I thought, trying to raise my spirits.

Fatigue weighed me down and I decided to stop for a short nap. However, I was now in a wide open grassland with very few trees for shade. It was noon and the blaring sun was not conducive to a nap. I laid down with my helmet covering my face like a cowboy would do with his hat, but it did not provide enough shade. A few miles further down the road, I managed to find a big shade tree that looked like a good nap spot. While it was shady and out of the sun, it was next to an almost stagnant creek and swarmed with bugs. For several minutes, I tried to close my eyes and ignore the bugs, but it was impossible.

Sleep would have to wait until evening. I couldn't catch a break on this day.

Riding on the road towards the Bannack Bench offered some wonderful views of the grasslands and mountains in the distance, as well as the thunderstorm headed directly for me. Nothing will get you out of the mental dumps like a close strike of lightning. I shifted into a higher gear and headed for the Cross Ranch, arriving just as the storm hit. No one answered when I knocked on the door of what looked like the main house. There were no people that I could see working around the house or the adjacent barns. I sat on the covered porch eating a snack and watching the storm's heavy raindrops fall as the wind blew hard enough to knock my bike over.

Finding refuge and barely beating a storm provided the break I had been looking for all day. With my spirits lifted, I was ready for more miles.

The remainder of the day was more of the same. Wide open cattle country, meandering dirt roads, and rolling hills. The grass covered hillsides provided open, big sky views for miles around.

My misery of the day finally relented. The joy of riding and experiencing new landscapes returned.

The final hurdle of the day was cresting Sheep Creek Divide, which involved a super steep pitch just before the top. I once again dismounted to push my loaded bike up the hill. This time, it was really the only option due to the grade of the incline. As I pushed over the top and saw miles and miles of open country laid out before me, I smiled for the first time that day.

Making it to the top meant a downhill would follow, and it was a mighty fun downhill. One that went down for miles without a single uphill section to navigate.

Ten miles outside of Lima, I stopped to camp for the night, even though it was still light out. For my own personal growth, I wanted to experience solo camping. I didn't want to go through the entire Tour Divide camping with others and staying in hotels. I found a flat patch of land less than 100 feet wide with the river on one side and the dirt road on the other. As I set up camp, I thought about the hearty breakfast I would enjoy when I reached Lima the next morning.

I set up camp, ate dinner, and settled into my comfy down cocoon before sunset. Since I had not slept for two nights and had trouble calming my mind for sleep, I took Advil PM. I slept so well that night, this became my new nighttime routine. They probably weren't needed every night; however, I wasn't willing to risk having more difficult days as a result of sleepless nights.

My first day of riding solo turned into my first night of camping solo. During the day, I enjoyed the solitude of riding after having dodged the thunderstorm. That evening, sleep came easily. What started out as the worst day of my race turned into a day that forced me to grow as both a racer and a person.

14

Enjoy the Moment

THE 100 MILES BETWEEN WARM RIVER and Sheep Creek Divide contained some of my lowest moments of the ride. In terms of mental mindset and overall fatigue, this was my worst stretch. Every pedal stroke became a challenge.

When I started the long gradual climb up Sheep Creek Divide, there were no more ranches, no more cars, and no more riders. It was just me and the road. I started to think about my friend Roger, who told me he knew I would keep going, even if there was pain or things got really difficult. It was only pain and it could always be fixed after the ride. Roger knew all about pain, having just been through knee replacement surgery on a knee that should have been replaced years earlier. He kept walking and working through pain that would have caused most people to become immobile.

Maybe he was simply giving me words of encouragement before the race. Maybe he saw in me a similar drive to fight through pain. Either way, his words popped into my head that day and helped to reset my mental state from one of feeling sorry for myself to one of motivation.

Was I really going to let a sore knee and lack of sleep get me down this much?

No. I was not.

I was willing to push my body to the breaking point to make sure I got to the finish in Antelope Wells, New Mexico. The goal of finishing was worth the hurt.

Out there on the lonely, dusty, washboard roads of Montana, my mindset shifted from thinking about suffering and ailments to enjoying the ride. I began to enjoy the moment.

I told myself, "Think about all of the people you know in the world. Will any of them ever be in this spot or on this road? Most likely not. So stop whining and enjoy the fact that you are out here living your dream."

It's a simple but powerful statement.

I repeated this each time I felt myself getting down, which was quite often that day, until I crested Sheep Creek Divide and rolled down the other side on the way to my first solo camping night. A few days later in Wyoming, I would find myself repeating the phrase once again as I hit a particularly tough mental stretch.

It had taken me over a week to get to this point. Was it pushing through some mental breaking points? Was it pushing through some physical barriers that would open my eyes to an entirely new experience? Was it finally being alone and having to look towards myself for motivation?

Probably a bit of all of these things came into play that day up on Sheep Creek Divide. Even though it's not a spectacular climb by Tour Divide measures, it's one I'll remember as the place where I changed my mindset and grew into a different version of myself.

Breaking down walls. Pushing through boundaries. Or as the text Brion sent me on that day said - "If you want to see the sunshine, you have to weather the storm." All three are ways of describing the process of perseverance and overcoming.

Many Tour Divide racers talk about it taking three or four days before they get into their long distance mindset. The same is true for backpackers starting a thru-hike of a long trail such as the Appalachian Trail or the Pacific Crest Trail. Due to the weather challenges of the first few days, my timeline stretched out to eight days. Prior to that, I was simply trying to survive by staying warm-ish and dry-ish as I rode. There was not much thought regarding routine or finding my endurance legs.

By the eighth day, the weather had broken, the mud had mostly dried, and I was riding solo. As I closed in on almost 1000 miles, my Tour Divide mindset was taking shape. No longer was I trying to survive each day. I was now driving forward with a new resolve.

I was finally enjoying the moment, and seeing the sunshine. New levels of possibility were before me.

It's like what happens when, as a kid, you have a teacher or a coach that pushes you way past the boundaries that you had placed around yourself and your abilities. It's not until you have to break through those limits that you realize there are other levels that you can achieve.

When I wrestled in high school, it was Coach Williamson that never let up on me. He was twice the size of me and the other lower weight class wrestlers. Yet he hammered us every practice until we could handle the onslaught while also using good techniques. His reasoning was that if we could endure what he dished out in practice, we would be prepared to win our match-es.

On the Tour Divide, it was my friends Roger and Brion that were my long distance virtual coaches. Or maybe it was more like they were my Obi-Wan Kenobi that would appear in my darkest times to guide me with their words of encouragement. I could hear their voices speaking to me as I rode.

"Keep going, it's only pain."

"See the sunshine."

By continuing to persevere and shift my mindset, the next day would become one of my finest days during the entire race.

PART TWO

Thrive

The difference between the impossible and the possible lies in a person's determination.

– TOMMY LASORDA

15

Two Breakfasts and a Missed Turn

M Y FINAL DAY IN MONTANA began with the first hints of light rising over the canyon walls at 5:30 a.m. Camping solo for the first time in the race with a full night's sleep (the first in three days) re-energized me. Even the bite of the cold mountain air as I climbed out of my cozy down bag could not dampen my spirits. As an added bonus, I looked forward to a hot breakfast in Lima, a mere twenty miles away. Woo hoo!

By the time I packed up my bike and started down the canyon, my hands were numb. The cold of the morning seeped into my core as I coasted down the hill. When the road flattened out twenty minutes later, my pedaling generated enough body heat to bring feeling back to my hands.

I was neatly tucked into my aero bars as the small town of Lima became visible in the distance. *Five more miles until breakfast* I told myself. To my left, trucks and cars zoomed by on the interstate. To my right, I caught a glimpse of a ranch set against the mountains. I saw the faintest hint of light clouds in an otherwise perfect blue sky. A bright red barn stood in contrast to the green fields, with the majestic snowcapped mountains behind. It was a postcard-worthy setting for a big sky Montana ranch. The large trees surrounding the house and barn were dwarfed by the peaks that rose out of the valley. Experiencing this setting while pedaling towards a hot breakfast was a stark contrast to the miserable miles I had endured just yesterday.

Only two hours into my day, and I had already enjoyed the comfort of solo camping, experienced stunning scenery, and now a sit-down breakfast awaited me in Lima. It was going to be a great day.

A left turn brought me under the interstate and into the town of Lima. The first building to the right was Jan's Cafe. Score! I'm a breakfast guy, and had been looking forward to my first "real" breakfast - the kind that includes eggs, bacon, and hash browns. Every other morning, my first food had been from a gas station and in a plastic wrapper.

On this morning, everything on the menu looked tasty, and I proceeded to order more than enough food. My feast of pancakes, eggs, bacon, biscuits & gravy, peaches, and plenty of hot coffee was one of the best meals of my life.

As I polished off the last bits of my breakfast, two racers walked into the restaurant. One was Scotty, whom I hadn't seen since Whitefish. The other rider I hadn't met before.

"Hey guys!" I said.

"Hey Andy!" Scotty replied. "Good to see you again. This is Ryan Lee. We've been riding together for a bit."

I shook Ryan's hand. "Nice to meet you. You guys doing ok?"

"Good until my rear wheel seized up. I'm waiting here for a replacement wheel. It's supposed to be here later today," Scotty said.

Ryan wasn't having the best of luck either. "I'm getting over bronchitis so the days have been rough, but I'm getting better."

"Hang in there. Y'all are riding great. We're almost through Montana," I said.

As much as I wanted to stay and keep talking, I knew I needed to get moving. Idaho called my name.

We said our goodbyes as they sat down to eat and I walked out of the restaurant and across the street to the gas station. Throughout the race, I enjoyed getting updates from fellow riders as our paths continued to cross.

Even after the ginormous breakfast, I remained on the prowl for food. I walked across the street to the gas station and bought enough food to fill my frame bag and gas tank bag. After calling home and checking in with my family, it was time to get back in the saddle and ride into Idaho.

Riding out of Montana is one of the big milestones on the Tour Divide. Almost everyone that makes it out of Montana finishes the race. Goodbye, Montana! I enjoyed your terrain and scenery, but it was time for a brief visit with Idaho.

The section from Lima into Idaho is perhaps the flattest portion of the route, other than the final 100 miles to the Mexican border. I wasn't complaining - the flat section gave my body a chance to recover. It was turning into a spectacular day.

Just as I was finding my pedaling rhythm while riding on the dirt road that parallels the winding Red Rock River, I came upon an elderly lady whose car was stopped on the side of the road.

The trunk was open and a spare tire was sitting on the ground behind the car.

"Hi there, do you need help?" I asked, as I came to a stop beside her car.

"Well, thank you, but my friend is coming to help."

Regardless of what she said, I wasn't going to just keep riding when she was all alone on the road. Growing up, my dad always stressed that we should stop and help people that are stranded. I had even done the same with my boys.

"I don't mind. I can change it for you."

I laid my bike down on the side of the road. With lug wrench in hand, I started to work on the last few lug nuts that she couldn't loosen. Good thing I ate such a big breakfast. It gave me the extra oomph and weight to get all of the lug nuts loose.

As I loosened the last nut, the man from town drove up and said he could finish the job. We talked for a few minutes. I got back on my bike and rode off with greasy hands. It felt good to help someone else after having other people be so kind and helpful to me during the race.

Climbing up a small incline, I rode past the Lima Reservoir dam where the terrain turns into a wide open meadow with mountains on either side. The miles flew by as I kept a nice pace. I stopped for a lunch of gas station snacks, and noticed storm clouds building behind me. It was time to get moving to see if I could outrun the storm. At this point in the race, I should have used the opportunity to save some energy and take it easy on my Achilles. Instead, I laid into the pedals and cranked up the pace. I was having a great day - my best day so far - and the clouds and rain were not going to catch me.

An eight-mile stretch of road headed due south, allowing the storm to gain ground on me. Glancing back towards the storm every few minutes, I saw the darkness and intensity building in the clouds.

Come on, pedal faster. Come on, don't let it catch you.

At an intersection, the route took a left turn, which brought be back to an eastern heading. That was my chance to stay ahead of the storm as the road passed by the Red Rocks Lake National Wildlife Refuge. The push of a tailwind helped propel me forward, yet the storm kept coming. It looked like I was going to be soaked before reaching the Idaho border.

Come on, pedal faster. Come on, you can beat this storm.

Generally, turns and intersections are desirable over a straight flat stretch of road, if for no other reason than to break up the monotony. As the road made a series of zigs heading north and zags heading east, I found myself wishing for the opposite. Each turn north brought the storm closer and an increase in the winds fighting against my progress. I pedaled hard when the next right turn heading east came into view.

Come on, pedal faster. Come on, it's only a few more miles.

Seven miles from the border, the route headed directly east for Idaho. By this time, a few light raindrops fell from the sky, and behind me I could see the rain clouds dropping rain across the valley. My route was now headed in the right direction, but there was a slight climb up to Red Rocks Pass to slow me down. I needed to bear down even more to stay on the dry edge of the storm.

Come on, pedal faster. Come on, make it to the border.

The spitting rain caught me a few times as my climbing speed dropped. Hitting a flatter spot, my pace pulled me a few feet outside of the first band of rain. It was touch and go.

Come on, pedal faster. Come on, pedal faster.

The storm beared down on me as I pushed on the pedals trying to reach the summit. After hours racing each other, we arrived at the summit together, and the raindrops began to fall on me. I stopped for a quick picture of my bike against the summit sign to document the milestone of riding through Montana.

Then it was time to fly down the hill and beat the storm once and for all. The downhill gave me the extra speed I needed to break away from the storm. It was not going to beat me. Not on this day.

Dirt gave way to pavement as I passed by Henry's Lake and several RV campgrounds. It was only a few miles further before I would reach Sawtelle Resort. The route followed a short section of trail that meandered through campgrounds and ATV trails. It was nice riding on trails instead of roads with traffic, so I settled in to enjoy some trail time through the trees.

Thanks to Jill Homer's book *Be Brave, Be Strong*, which documents her 2008 Tour Divide race, and perusing the ACA maps, I knew there was a Subway restaurant at the resort. I planned to celebrate my victory over the storm with a couple of sandwiches.

As I rolled up to the Subway, a line from the movie Tommy Boy kept running through my head.

"That. Was. Awesome!"

The day had been awesome indeed. And it wasn't even finished. I had conquered solo camping on the Divide and outrun a thunderstorm. Since good things always come in threes, conquering the infamous thirty miles of Rail Trail became my next challenge.

After pushing so hard during the day, I easily devoured a foot long chicken and a six inch veggie sub. The sandwiches were a welcome change from the boatload of sugary foods I consumed each day. Refueled and re-energized, I was ready to tackle the Rail Trail which began a few miles down the road from Sawtelle. The Rail Trail is not an ideal bike trail - straight and extremely sandy, with small undulations that make it hard to find a rhythm. On this Saturday afternoon, there was a fair amount of ATV traffic. I'm sure they wondered why a cyclist would be on such a trail.

I wondered the same thing about them. A straight trail where the ATVs and bicycles went about the same speed because of the bumps doesn't seem all that fun for anyone. For a time, my speed matched the vehicle in front of me, and I ingested more than enough exhaust fumes. They turned off a few miles outside of the main resort area, and I was left to ride the Rail Trail in solitude - with the exception of the cows in the middle of the road a few miles further on. The combination of the wetlands and the setting sun made for some great pictures. Stopping to take in the trees, the reflection of the sun off of the water, and the colors of the sunset also gave me a chance to take pressure off of my numb hands.

Overall, the Rail Trail wasn't "horrible" (as my son has been known to say when talking about another student's artwork at school). Enjoyable? No. Tolerable? For one time, yes. Settling into a rhythm, admitting torture but not defeat, and accepting the Rail Trail for what it was got me through the thirty miles. I managed to find a gear that allowed me to pedal smoothly, even in the deep sandy sections, without having to push too hard on the pedals. Even my Achilles were happy.

However, my hands did not fare so well. To make it through the endless bumps and deep sand, I gripped the handlebars tighter than normal, putting extra pressure on my hands. By the end of the Rail Trail, the numbness covered everything but my thumbs.

A tunnel marked the end of the Rail Trail. The deep sand and bumps vanished, replaced by several miles of hard-packed trail that gently dropped to Warm River below. Evening was descending on Idaho. My legs felt good, and I could have continued riding. However, my analytical mind was already set on stopping for the night.

When I began riding that morning, I mentally set the Warm River Campground as my destination. It's almost impossible to reach a self-imposed goal, and then tell yourself you're going to keep riding. Looking back, I should have kept riding. I wasn't tired, and the next thirty miles afforded plenty of opportunities for stealth camping along the forest roads.

The campground was full of families and mosquitoes, those pesky bugs that can drive any animal or person mad. I'm referring to the mosquitoes, not the families. The families were nice to see. It made me think of camping with my own two boys, and how much I missed them.

The campers were having fun, enjoying running around, campfires, hot meals, and a beer or two for the parents. I ate a solitary dinner of more sugary gas station food. With the mosquitoes swarming, I ate quickly, trying to fit in a lot of calories before I went to sleep. I zipped myself into my bivy to keep the mosquitoes away, while everyone around me continued to enjoy the early evening. Thanks to a little help from Advil PM and my ear plugs, I fell asleep before dark, even as the kids played loudly in the campsites around me.

I awoke to a calm sunrise, a great way to start the day. The beautiful colors and the quiet of the morning more than made up for the cold temperatures. I was ready to ride out of Idaho and into wonderful Wyoming. The state gets a bad rap from most riders. I was looking forward to the variety of terrain, the wild camping, and long days of open views. Wyoming also had the Great Divide Basin which was another unique piece of the Tour Divide I was excited to experience.

Packing up a tarp and sleeping gear while the rest of the campground is fast asleep makes you realize how loud all of your lightweight camping gear can be. I tried to be as quiet as possible as I packed up and rode out of the campground. A left turn onto pavement and then a quick climb warmed me up. I enjoyed seeing the wildlife that had also gotten an early start to the morning, spotting a couple of raccoons and a fox in the first few miles. The pavement leveled out as it took me through a few small farms, making for easy morning riding. My focus zeroed in on Squirrel Creek Ranch, which offered the promise of a hot breakfast. That would make two hot breakfasts in a row - music to my ears (and my stomach).

Along these roads, the Tetons came into the view for the first time. Wyoming was getting closer.

Reaching Squirrel Creek, everything appeared to be closed. I tried the front door, which was locked, and started to feel defeated. It was like Ernest Thayer's *Casey at the Bat* and I had just struck out. I began digging through my gas tank bag in search of my next meal. As I looked at my options, I heard someone say, "Good morning!"

I looked up to see an elderly man standing in the front door. "Morning! I thought you were closed."

"No, come on in. I'll make you some breakfast," he said.

I leaned my bike against a fence and walked into the house. "Thank you so much. I know it's early on a Sunday morning."

"I don't mind. Let me wake my grandson up, and then we'll get you something to eat."

After pulling his grandson out of bed, he came back and asked, "Will scrambled eggs, hash browns, bacon, and toast be okay?"

"Yes sir, that would be great!"

"Would you like coffee too?"

"Yes, please," I said.

The grandfather left me in the main room, and soon I heard food preparations begin in his kitchen. As I sat at the counter, I took in my surroundings. It appeared that the heart of Squirrel Creek Ranch was the grandfather's house, where he lived on the property. He added a few cabins out back, as well as a campground. While I had different expectations based on the information in the ACA maps, I could not complain. I enjoyed the non-commercial, small business places more than a big chain restaurant.

"Thank you. Are you working this summer for your grandfather?" I asked the grandson, as he placed the first hot cup of coffee in front of me.

"Yeah, I go back to school in the fall."

"This looks like a nice place to spend the summer. Sorry I woke you up early."

"It's ok. My grandfather never lets me sleep too late," he said with a faint smile.

Pans and dishes clanked as the grandfather whipped up my breakfast. The smell of sizzling bacon wafted from the kitchen.

Just minutes ago, I faced disappointment at the prospect of having to eat another candy bar. Now I sat with coffee in hand and a hearty meal on its way. Tour Divide fortunes change in the blink of an eye.

The grandfather brought out a plate piled high with enough food for two meals. As I dug into the crispy hash browns, I was taken back to sitting at my grandparent's table in South Carolina. I could almost see my grandfather sitting across from me, stirring creamer into his coffee, and sopping up the remnants of his breakfast with a biscuit.

"More coffee?" the grandfather asked, snapping me back to the present.

"Yes, please. One more cup."

"Where are you headed today?" he asked.

"Past Yellowstone and then on towards Pinedale."

"That's a long way to go. Need more food?"

"No sir, this is more than plenty and I have a lot packed on my bike," I said. "Thank you so much. I appreciate you cooking this up for me."

"You're welcome. Glad I heard you outside before you rode off."

"Me too!" I said with a smile.

After thanking the grandfather and grandson yet again, I paid and pedaled towards Flagg Ranch. The road was wide with gentle hills and very little traffic. The only traffic was a group of horse drawn wagons that were used as part of a nightly Western cookout. Four hours later, I arrived at Flagg Ranch, hungry for lunch.

Unfortunately, Flagg Ranch turned out to be the complete opposite of Squirrel Creek Ranch. While the food was good, the service in the restaurant was slow and inattentive. Over at the convenience store, the attendant practically threw all of my precious sugar-laden snacks at me after he rang me up. I did meet a couple who were riding cross country on folding bikes, and I enjoyed talking with them. However, the rest of my stay in Flagg Ranch felt like a bust.

While the morning started out great, I allowed my experience at Flagg Ranch and a tougher-than-expected pavement climb to put me in a bad mood. The road probably wasn't as steep as it felt, and the service probably wasn't as bad as I thought. Instead of getting frustrated, I should have taken it in stride, been happy I had food and water, and continued riding down the road. It really is important to keep a happy mind and not let things get you down.

The road, full of RVs out on their summer vacations, climbed towards the Tetons. As I pedaled up the hill, I met two Continental Divide Trail (CDT) hikers forced to come out of the mountain trails and on to the road due to high snow. Stopping to talk to them and hear about their own adventure helped to reset my mind and put me in a much better mood.

Taking in the view of the Tetons was special, even though I had first seen them back in high school. After days of being unable to view the landscape, the Tetons were a beautiful and welcome sight. It was overcast with dark clouds rolling in. The lake and the jagged mountains made for a wonderful photo. I couldn't linger long because I had miles to go if I wanted to get over Togwotee Pass.

The route turned off the highway, passing by Turpin Meadows Campground. It then led to a dirt road, which turned into doubletrack up Togwotee Pass. The twenty miles between Turpin Meadows and Togwotee Pass were brutal for me - lots of steep climbs and walking.

When I finally made it back to Highway 287 for the final pitch to the summit, I thought I was in the clear. Nope. My energy was gone. I was once again left walking up a paved road. With the pain in my ankles and a lack of motivation, I couldn't turn over the pedals, even though I was riding in my easiest gear. Never, in all of my planning for the race, did I envision walking my bike on the side of a highway.

After finally cresting the pass, I mounted my bike and started flying down the hill. I glanced down at my GPS, and was perplexed that it said I was not on route. This was the highway, the highway that led to the next climb of Union Pass. I stopped, dug out my map, and realized my mistake. The Tour Divide route took a dirt road turnoff at the summit, navigating around Brooks Lake instead of taking the highway.

It was a good thing I checked my GPS when I did so I could correct my mistake. Going off-route would have resulted in an automatic disqualification from the race. At that moment, I wasn't feeling the joy in discovering my mistake. Cranky, angry, and grumpy is a more accurate description. The Lava Mountain Lodge was waiting for me at the bottom of the hill just a few miles away. Instead, I had to climb a mile back up the mountain and take some stupid dirt road to get to the lodge.

Turns out, the dirt road wasn't much of a road. After a bit of searching, I found it traversing away from the highway and completely covered in snow. All I could do was push my bike through the snow, making me even more cranky. I yelled at the trail. I wanted the snow and mud to stop.

It didn't.

I turned onto the north side of the mountain, greeted by more snow and mud. The road eventually dropped below the snow line, leaving plenty of mud to contend with. That's when I looked up and took in the stunning view of Pinnacle Butte. It was worth every bit of the snow, mud, and frustration to get there. The afternoon sun perfectly highlighted the pinnacles in the distance. The sheer walls of rock towered over the deep green of the pine and spruce trees that grew from the shores of Brooks Lake up to the edge of the cliffs.

The view brought me back to the "enjoy the moment" thoughts I had while I was climbing up Sheep Creek Divide on my way towards Lima, Montana. "Shut up and quit whining," I kept telling myself. "When would anyone you know be on this road and have a chance to witness this scenic beauty? Probably never."

With a much clearer mind and in a happier state, I made it back to the highway. I cruised into the Lava Mountain Lodge, which had food, hotel rooms, campsites, and bunkhouses. My intent was to camp that night, but the single room cabin option was too good to pass up. For a few extra dollars, I had a bed, table, electricity, and heat. After check-in, I ate my dinner in my room, took a shower, and stood around a campfire talking with the family that ran the lodge.

The day brought me from Idaho into Wyoming. It started with a grandfather and grandson at breakfast in Idaho. It ended 120 miles and 7500 feet of climbing later, with another family around a campfire in Wyoming. A mostly enjoyable day filled with thoughts of my own family.

16

Thinking of Family

A S I RODE OUT OF Montana, through Idaho, and into Wyoming, my thoughts turned to my family.

'Eating breakfast in Lima and then stopping to help someone with a flat tire had me thinking about my dad, who would soon be flying out to meet me at the finish.

My dad ran his own business, and my brother and I helped out after school and on Saturdays. He worked six days a week for more than forty years, selling and delivering portable storage buildings. Being the youngest, I was the gofer for hammers, boards, and pipes used to move the buildings during delivery.

We worked in the heat of the South Carolina summers, the humid cold of winter, and plenty of rainy days. It wasn't glamorous work by any means. It was character-building work that I now appreciate, even if at the time I was a grumpy kid that wanted to go play in the woods instead of working.

Through all of the hard work, my dad always fed us well. We'd start with breakfast, often a ham biscuit or biscuits and gravy at Hardee's. In the afternoon, there was a snack of boiled peanuts from Berley's, the bar next door, or a milkshake from Hite's Dairy Bar. Even now, we still have a connection over breakfast. When my family travels back to South Carolina, breakfast with my dad is always a highlight of our visit.

My dad fed us, made us work, taught us by example, and told some really bad jokes. On more than one occasion, he stopped to help someone with a flat tire. That's why I felt so obligated to help the woman outside of Lima with her flat tire that day. Once I saw her situation, I had to help.

The day after staying in the Wise River Campground had me remembering my granddaddy because of the grandfather and grandson that so graciously fed me at Squirrel Creek Ranch that morning. It was a classic working man's breakfast of eggs, toast, hash browns, and bacon, with plenty of coffee and orange juice to wash it all down. One that my grandfather would have enjoyed.

During the forty miles of rolling hills between Squirrel Creek Ranch and Yellowstone, I spent a lot of time thinking of my own grandfather, who passed away more than twenty years ago when I was a teenager. The hearty breakfast and the grandfatherly presence made it all too easy to picture myself back in South Carolina, sitting in my grandparent's kitchen. Each summer, my brother and I spent a week at their house, following my granddaddy around as he tended to his hunting dogs and worked on his bulldozer. He always let me have a small cup of coffee, and occasionally a small puff on his cigar when my grandmother wasn't looking.

My thoughts centered around being in the moment that morning. The pace was comfortable, the views of the Tetons slowly came into view, and I enjoyed the ride.

My grandfather never got to travel and experience the places I visited during the race. As a young man, he shipped off to Europe for WWII, but that's not the kind of trip one looks forward to taking. He came back from the war, settled down, and rarely left his small town.

Here I was taking a month off from work to ride my bike in the mountains. As I rode, I realized how grateful I was for the experience. I was lucky to be living out my dream, something my grandfather (and probably many in his generation) never got to do.

A few months before the Tour Divide, my wife, my two boys, and I went back to South Carolina to see my family. My brother had just moved into a new house and finally had his dream workshop. While showing me around, my brother came across two King Edward cigar boxes. My granddaddy used to give us the empty cigar boxes to store pencils, rocks, and other small items we had at home. Man, we loved those boxes.

I picked up one of the boxes and was instantly transported back to my grandfather's shop. I could almost smell the grease, see his old green truck, and hear his hunting dogs out back. The thirty-year-old cigar box was in rough shape - discolored, the cardboard fraying at the edges - but it was perfect to me.

Opening it, I found two cigars still in the box. How had they remained in the box all these years later? My brother let me take that box and cigars back home to Colorado, and it was immediately placed in my office where I could see it every day. It's still there even now.

One of the cigars was on my Tour Divide packing list. I planned to smoke it when I reached the border. But more importantly, it would be something from my childhood and family that would travel with me along the route. In the end, I decided to leave the cigar at home. My granddaddy was in my heart and that's how he would go along the route with me.

17

The Big, Bad Basin

NESTLED IN MY CABIN WITH heat, electricity, a table, and bunk bed, sleep came easily that night. However, in the morning, something was missing - my desire to get on my bike and ride all day. My morning routine was much slower than usual. Breakfast in my cabin (a Coke and cinnamon roll from the lodge store) was much more relaxed than on my previous mornings. Eventually, I packed up everything and it was time to leave Lava Mountain. Instead of being on the road at first light, I managed to dilly-dally long enough for the front desk to make a 7:00 a.m. pot of coffee.

As I finished my second cup, Ryan Lee rolled up. I first met Ryan back in Lima, Montana, and had not seen another rider since. The original 150 racers were now spread out across multiple states, with the leader well into Colorado and the last place racer still in Montana.

We chatted a bit about how each of us were feeling on this cold morning. Ryan wore all of his warm clothing, having just come down the long downhill after Togwotee Pass. Like me, he missed the turn onto the Brooks Lake Road, but unfortunately he had not realized his mistake until he had ridden all the way down to Lava Mountain. He was now contemplating his next move. I felt really bad for him. Even though he was frozen from the long downhill after an early morning start, he was determined to ride the official route. I suggested he find a ride back to the top of the pass, alleviating the need to grind back up on his own power. I wished him good luck, amazed at Ryan's integrity to make sure he did things the right way, and I headed off to start the ride towards Union Pass.

Ryan is one of the unsung heroes of a race like the Tour Divide. Never at the front, but pushing himself past his limits, suffering day in and day out, and always racing with integrity. I found out that he managed to get a ride back to the top of the pass, where he got back on the official route. Ryan had been battling bronchitis since the third day of the race, yet he still pushed himself to get up very early each morning and ride 100 mile days. Unfortunately, he had to pull out due to the bronchitis soon after Pinedale, Wyoming. I'm still amazed by his ride and I wish he could have finished the race.

Leaving Lava Mountain Lodge, I descended several miles on pavement. The route took a right turn off the highway and ascended Union Pass - the last big climb in Wyoming. It's a long climb and very steep for the first few miles. The climb was hard but enjoyable, and I found a groove that had been missing for several days. I was having a great day on the bike. In just a few hours I went from dragging my feet to riding strong on Union Pass. It was a happy change, and one I feel was partly due to running into Ryan and watching him tackle his own challenges that morning.

The climb leveled out a bit after a few miles. At that point, I looked back towards the Tetons and Yellowstone. The high vista and crystal clear blue skies provided a magnificent view. I could also see the Cathedral Mountains - the ones that annoyed and frustrated me the previous day on Brooks Lake Road. Seeing those mountains in the early morning sunshine put a smile on my face and made my legs feel even stronger.

There was one patch of snow at the top of Union Pass that required walking. After pushing through the snow, I met a motorcycle rider going northbound all the way to the Arctic.

"Good morning, how are you?" he asked.

"Doing good. This is a long climb."

"How much snow have you found on the way up?"

"This is the only patch. How is the other side of the climb?" I asked.

"All clear. I camped a few miles back last night. It was cold up here," he replied.

"Where are you headed?"

"Up to Alaska. Started out six days ago at the Mexican border."

"That's where I'm headed! But it will take me a lot more than six days," I said.

"It's beautiful out here."

"Sure is. The views are amazing."

"Well, enjoy your ride south. Watch out for grizzlies," he advised.

"I will. And have a great ride up to Alaska," I replied as I hopped on my bike and pedaled away.

He went north and I continued south towards Pinedale, with the downhill of Union Pass and thirty miles of pavement in between.

Incredible views greeted me at the top of Union Pass. Bright blue skies met vibrant green grass, with mountains and alpine lakes in between. A postcard view for sure. The sunlight glittered on the small alpine lakes. The myriad of spruce trees lining the meadow gave way to steep mountains, which soared above tree line, and ended in snow covered peaks.

The vistas at the top of the climbs made the struggle to reach them worth the effort. What made them even better was being there all by myself to take in the beauty nature had to offer. My snacks at the summits were some of the best of the entire ride, even if they happened to be a crushed Fig Newton and a melted candy bar.

While the climb up Union Pass was steep and continuous, the downhill was much different, but not in a good way. First, there was a rolling summit that went on for miles, which meant more climbing when I was ready for the official downhill. Several unnerving "Grizzly Bears Active" signs were posted beside the road. The signs didn't say "Be Bear Aware" like the other signs encountered since Banff. No, they specifically said there were active grizzlies in the area. I kept riding, on high alert, and hoped I didn't run into any grizzlies.

After miles of rollers and more climbing than I expected after reaching the "summit" marked on my GPS, the downhill eventually materialized. However, the deep ruts and large rocks littering the road took away all of the downhill fun. The numbness in my hands grew worse. That last holdouts, my thumbs, were succumbing to the beating dished out by the road.

I was happy to reach the bottom and hit pavement, where I anticipated a smooth gradual coast into Pinedale. Instead, I found an undulating road that dashed my hopes of easy miles into town.

The ACA map indicated a store located between Union Pass and Pinedale, and I looked forward to the opportunity to stop there. Sitting down to drink a Coke would have felt so good, but it was not to be. The store was closed on Mondays, and I happened to be riding past it on a Monday. In the grand scheme of things, it wasn't a big deal since I had plenty of water and food to reach Pinedale. It's just another example of me thinking too much while out on the ride.

It was early afternoon when I arrived in Pinedale with ninety miles completed for the day. I enjoyed a late lunch, ordering a bacon cheeseburger and fries with a little vegetable soup thrown in for variety. Even with hours of sunlight left and re-supply options galore, I decided to call it a day. In my pre-race planning, I identified several short days to give me a buffer if I was running behind schedule. Pinedale was the destination for one of those short days. Good for planning, bad for racing.

The planning helped me understand mileages between towns and set goals for each day. In hindsight, I became too fixated with my Tour Divide plan, letting my pre-race goals become the only thing I wanted to accomplish for the day. I should have identified the towns coming up for re-supply options without setting a hard and fast endpoint for each day. Go with the flow, rather than having such a rigid plan.

After talking myself into staying in Pinedale, I checked into a hotel conveniently located next door to a Subway and gas station. Each day, the pain and soreness in my ankles worsened, so finding everything in one location was a nice benefit. I walked gingerly across the parking lot and into the gas station to purchase sunscreen, breakfast for the next morning, and plenty of snacks. Next, I moseyed over from the gas station counter to the in-store Subway where I ordered two Subway sandwiches - my typical 6" veggie, plus a 6" steak and cheese. I knew from experience, once I checked in to the hotel, I wouldn't want to leave again until morning. Nothing like Subway sandwiches and chips in your hotel room for dinner.

Since this was my first hotel stay in five days, I decided to wash my clothes. The last time they had been freshly laundered (ok, simply rinsed out with some water) was back in Helena. Oh man, they really needed it. Washing them right in the tub, the water quickly changed from clear to black with loads of sand and dirt mixed in. Those were some dirty clothes. I can't imagine how clothes look and smell for the leaders at the end of the race; those riders typically do not stop long enough to wash their clothes.

With clean clothes, it was time to clean myself up. Gotta be clean before tackling the Great Basin, right? Stepping out of the shower, I caught a glimpse of myself in the mirror and became a little worried. It looked like I had lost a lot of weight, especially in my upper body and arms. Even while riding 100 miles per day, I did not develop a voracious appetite, so I never ate two meals at a sitting like other riders. It was time to pay more attention to my calorie intake and make sure I ate extra food at night. A few hundred calories before going to bed would aid my recovery and ensure I had enough energy to keep going day after day. It was a good thing my latest gas station haul included some extra food. I did my best to eat as much of it that night as I could.

The remedy for my other ailments was not so easy. My Achilles were not getting better. The numbness in my hands covered all of my fingers. Added to these was a new issue - the big toenail on my left foot was a lovely shade of purple. The pressure from wearing my cycling shoes all day, every day was taking its toll.

The alarm woke me before sunrise. With a clean cycling kit, lots of food, and an excitement about reaching the Basin later that day, I took off in the darkness. On the paved road to Boulder, Wyoming, the sun began to rise over the mountains, bringing the first colors of the day. Many oil and gas vehicles passed by me as they went to start their day at the well sites. The route turned left onto State Highway 353. Of course, my bike veered left just before the turn-off, into the gas station in search of fresh hot coffee. There was nothing I could do to stop the bike. The cashier even gave me the coffee for free since that was all I was purchasing. This day had already started on the right foot.

Fueled up on coffee, I pedaled towards the Wind River mountains in the distance as the sunlight brightened the morning sky. The highway eventually turned to dirt just before the Lander Cutoff Road. I read that Lander, Wyoming was the gateway into the Wind River Range, a favorite spot for many mountaineers and backpackers. Even though the mountains were at least twenty miles in the distance, I began to understand why they were so loved.

The dirt road was flanked by sagebrush and the occasional lonely tree. Further out, the rolling foothills were covered in the dark green of pine and spruce trees. Looking even higher, I was drawn to the jagged profile of the mountains, still covered by snow. Above the mountains, wispy clouds floated in a light blue sky. Each time I crested a small climb, the expanse of snow capped mountains popped into view.

This became one of my favorite sections of the ride. My view that morning was calm, quiet, and peaceful. Over a four hour stretch that paralleled the Wind River Range, less than five cars passed by. The road was mine to enjoy and soak in the tranquility provided by the Winds. Everything aligned for another one of those moments that will never fade from my memory.

I stopped to take my lunch break atop the Continental Divide. To the left, the Winds still soared into the sky. To the right, cattle ranches, small creeks lined with cottonwood trees, and the expanse of open Wyoming stretched out to the horizon. For some, sitting atop a high mountain peak or looking up at the majesty of the Canadian Rockies might have provided a better perch for lunch, but I'm not so sure. For my happy spot, I keep coming back to a lonely dirt road cutting through Sublette County Wyoming.

Eventually, the dirt road gave way to pavement as the route traversed its way north towards Atlantic City, Wyoming. After crossing the Sweetwater River, I began several miles of climbing on super-smooth newly laid asphalt. Along this section, I caught up with Sarah Caylor, whom I had not seen since Ovando. We rode the final five miles to South Pass City, passing by what little was left of the once-bustling gold mining town and it's Carissa Gold Mine.

A few miles further down the road, from the top of a hill, we spotted the few buildings that make up the tiny town of Atlantic City in the valley below. Even though the town's population is only fifty people, Atlantic City is one of the most important stops along the race route, the final place to re-supply before the

Great Basin and its 140 mile stretch of nothingness. A split in the Continental Divide forms the Great Basin, causing no water to flow into the area between Atlantic City and Rawlins. Within the Great Basin, there are no houses, few roads, and only the occasional oil well to hint at a human presence.

Atlantic City boasts one bar and one café, both known for keeping irregular hours. Sarah and I timed our arrival perfectly, finding the café open for a late lunch. Many a Tour Divide rider has faced the opposite situation, arriving when everything was closed. The rider must choose between staying overnight to wait for something to open the following day, or tackling the Great Basin without enough food, and more importantly, water. Given the unpredictable headwinds that can reduce speeds to a walking pace, a rider needs to carry enough food and water to last up to a full day.

I ordered two PB&J sandwiches to-go for my dinner, and gathered a few other snacks and drinks from the small selection on the shelves in the corner. I left town that afternoon with a frame bag full of food, four liters of water, a Coke, and a Gatorade. My timing gave me the opportunity to camp in the Great Basin, which was one of my goals coming into the race. That is, if I could make it out of Atlantic City.

The road out of town is uphill and STEEP! Super steep. I decided to walk almost all of the hill since there was no use in pushing myself too hard right after a break. Sarah impressively rode the entire climb, grinding up the steepest sections at a slow but steady pace. After cresting the top of the hill, the desolate Basin was laid out before us. No one had rolled out the red carpet for us. It was more like the dirty bar mat that has been stepped on and spilled on and thrown out into the alley to dry.

All that my eyes saw was the barren area in front of me, with rolling hills, lots of grasses, and various shades of brown.

While the landscape was anything but lush, the tailwind that blew us deeper into the Basin was a welcomed companion. At times, it felt like there were miles between pedal strokes as the road gradually descended and the wind propelled us forward. It was fun riding to say the least. While the miles flew by, the clouds building from the west were darkening, forecasting tougher miles to come that evening.

In our giddiness of enjoying the tailwind, we flew past the one water well marked on the map. Sarah carried a lot less water than me into this desolate stretch. We navigated deeper into the Basin, riding up and over many hills. Given the name, one would think the Basin is a flat expanse. The reality is that it contains plenty of shorter climbs after the initial twenty miles of easy roads. At the bottom of one such hill, the maps identified Arapahoe Creek as a good water source unless it has been a dry year. Given all of the water we encountered up to this point in the race, it did not seem like a dry year. However, the stream bed was dry, except for a few putrid algae-filled puddles. Sarah's small amount of water would have to last her much longer than she had anticipated.

As the sun began to set, a thunderstorm was building all around us. Lightning could be seen in multiple directions. The oncoming storm tightened its grip on us and would soon clamp down on the small area of dry land we rode through. The wind picked up, making for even faster miles. Instead of enjoying the pace, I began to worry about shelter from the storm in an area that provided very little natural shelter. Riding through rain is one thing. Riding through a thunderstorm at night is a completely different animal. We came upon a large section of snow fence just as the winds really started whipping.

As darkness fell, I made my decision. My campsite would be next to the snow fence to provide as much shelter as possible from the storm. Sarah wanted to ride on to get at least halfway through the Basin since she was running very low on water. We talked a bit about our plans, and she reluctantly made the same decision as me to stay at the snow fence. We set up our tents, although it was more like we tried to hold onto thin lightweight materials as poles and stakes were hastily put into the ground, as the wind grew stronger and stronger behind the fence. If my tarp had come out of my grip while setting up, it would have sailed off into the distance, never to be found again. We both managed to set up our shelters and crawl inside as the rain began to fall.

After stopping early for the storm and the difficulty setting up camp, the storm turned out to be a dud, lasting for only a few minutes. In hindsight, I should have kept riding, especially since the next morning's winds shifted into a headwind. The experience of the first week of rain, snow, and cold definitely impacted my decisions that night.

However, I was happy, dry, and warm in my shelter that night, so I really can't complain. It had been a great Tour Divide day - beautiful vistas, good road conditions, good company, another hot meal, coffee, and a tailwind. It doesn't get much better than that on the Tour Divide.

18

Goals

GOING INTO THE TOUR DIVIDE, my one true objective was simply finishing the race, doing whatever it took to ride myself to the finish in whatever time I could muster. Outside of that, I had three other goals for experiences during the race:

1. Ride the Fleecer downhill.
2. Camp in the Basin.
3. Eat pie in Pie Town.

By the end of my twelfth day of the race, the first two goals were complete, with only the lure of pie remaining on my checklist. The goals had been tough to accomplish, which was to be expected. Given my history with weather on rides, a cold night ride down Fleecer and a thunderstorm with high winds in the Basin were really not all that bad.

In my mind, I had this idyllic notion of riding into the Basin in the late afternoon, finding a flat campsite where I could eat my dinner and then cowboy camp; no shelter, just me in my sleeping bag under the Wyoming stars.

Didn't happen.

The only part of that vision that became reality was eating dinner in the Basin.

Goals are kind of like the picture of people we create in our minds. Rarely does the picture match reality when we meet that person for the first time. So why was I dreaming up goals in my head, knowing full well that reality would be much different? The Tour Divide was already hard enough. Why make it harder and more stressful by introducing goals?

It may well be that I'm a little crazy. However, I think it also has to do with how I'm wired. Bikepacking and cycling are only one half of me. The other half is an engineer that's very analytical. These halves are definitely at odds on many occasions. One wants to go out to see the world and live a simple existence. The other wants to plan and prepare for how everything will play out while using technology and science to optimize efficiency.

More often than not, the analytical side wins out with me. That means the simple existence my bikepacking/adventure side desires where each day is taken as it comes is not often found. Instead, I wake up planning, iterating through ideas, and over-thinking each part of the day.

It's not necessarily a good or a bad thing. Instead, it's just me and it's something I've come to accept. Back in high school, splitting time between my nerdy and athletic endeavors was a challenge. As an adult, it brought me to bikepacking. Yes, the analytical side of me really enjoys the sport of bikepacking because I can use my planning and logic to find an optimized way to carry gear, calories, and setup for each day, while also letting me use technology for navigation and lighting systems.

While preparing for the Tour Divide, I had spreadsheets of gear weights and load distributions and mileage charts. It was a nerd's dream. In between all of that, the adventurous side was able to go on long rides in the woods and see plenty of scenery and sunsets. It was a perfect match of my two seemingly unrelated personalities.

So the half nerd, half adventure mindsets found a combination that worked. Of course, my wife would say it was always a perfect combination, and one that swept her off her feet upon first sight. Well, I may have gotten a little carried away there. Get it? Carried away, swept off her feet!

Anyway, back to the goals and why my analytical side needed them.

Having goals actually makes it easier for me from a mental perspective. Without them, my mind would be wandering aimlessly while it tried to come up with a plan of its own. Plus, plans and goals are what motivated me to keep going forward. Rather than waste mental cycles and stress on worrying about a plan, having something in place from the outset works much better for me. Simply riding my bike 2700 miles with the singular goal of reaching Antelope Wells was not enough. I needed intermediate goals to occupy my mind, even when they unfolded differently that I had originally planned.

All of this may sound crazy if you are not an analytical person, and understandably so. It's like the people I saw at the start of the race that were trying to figure out how their GPS worked for the first time. My head would have exploded if that had been me in that situation. They simply took it in stride and were not really worried.

Yes, it may sound like this analytical brain thing is a big mess of trouble to deal with. In some regards, that would be an understatement. At other times, like making sure I didn't run out of water, it's a blessing.

In the end, one way is not better than the other. My preparation allowed me to think about goals and plans and more plans. The riders that went by the seat of their pants had plenty of time to think about where the next water re-supply or food would come from as they rode. Either way, riders pedal towards New Mexico.

Now, the bigger goals that took a week or more to reach were a good idea. Rather than being some type of arbitrary daily target, they were experiences that would be encountered during the race. They pushed me moving forward, keeping my mind active as I thought about how a scenario would play out for me to reach a destination. Because the goals were experience-based, they were concrete, but not set in stone on a timeline.

Dreaming of camping in the Basin was a perfectly fine goal. If it happened, great. If the timing worked out where I rode through the Basin during the day, I would have kept riding and not really worried about the missed opportunity. The experience of the Basin would have still been there even if the goal to spend the night there wasn't realized.

Same for Fleecer Ridge. I had to go down the steep hill one way or the other to complete the route. So why not make it fun and test my technical abilities? If I crashed trying, at least I could say I gave it a try before picking up the carnage from falling on such a steep slope and walking down to the bottom.

But the short term goal of reaching a certain town or campsite for the day? That turned out to be a bad idea - I let that one goal dictate my actions for the day rather than simply going out for a ride. If I didn't reach that goal, I over-analyzed the reasons why I didn't reach a given location. If I reached it early, instead of continuing to ride, my drive was empty because I had achieved a goal.

I wish I could have been more like Dan Hensley, my riding companion on the first day, and just go with the flow. He was very good at taking things as they came, greatly reducing his stress levels if something changed, whether good or bad. As the race went on, I got a little better at going with the flow. At least, better for me, which was still way below what riders like Dan could manage.

My stubborn streak, the one that caused my mom to break my crayons and tear out pages from my coloring book, was somewhat of an antidote to the analytical side that wanted to make goals for everything. This was especially true on the bad days that didn't go according to my plan. I happily let my stubbornness push me further and harder than I should have, simply to make some arbitrary goal I had set at the beginning of the day.

The battle between my analytical side and my outdoor adventure side, with that stubborn streak wrapped all around them, would never be completed. It would continue to be waged with each sunrise, town, and sunset along the way.

Only one experience goal remained on my list. Pie Town was still over 1000 miles away. After traveling that far, the pie was going to be oh-so-tasty.

Or would it? Would I even make it to Pie Town? Would they be open when I got there? In my mind, I envisioned sitting down to two pieces of pie, a couple of scoops of vanilla ice cream, and a hot cup of coffee.

In order to find out, I first had to get out of the Basin and Wyoming.

19

A Bowl Full of Cherries

AS THE SUNLIGHT FILTERED THROUGH my tarp, I opened my eyes to a beautiful calm sunrise casting the sky in a light blue hue highlighted with soft pink clouds. A major contrast to the angry sky that forced us to camp early the night before.

I had successfully camped in the Basin. While I would have preferred cowboy camping with just my sleeping bag under a star filled sky, I could still check off one of my Tour Divide goals.

"Hey Andy, I'm going to ride ahead because I'm out of water," Sarah yelled over to my campsite. She was already packed up and headed out for the day.

"Ok, sounds good. Hope you find water soon," I replied as I crawled out of my sleeping bag.

I downed a Coke - my morning caffeine fix in the Basin - and ate a PB&J sandwich for breakfast as I packed my campsite back onto the bike. I was ready for more Basin riding. Overnight the winds had shifted. Yesterday's glorious tailwind was now a moderate headwind, more of a nuisance than one of those monster headwinds that are notorious in the Basin.

A few miles down the road, I ran into a group of five guys, probably in their early twenties, camping around an old wagon. Tarps and gear were pitched all around the wagon with all of the guys smiling as they sat in their warm down jackets, making breakfast and sipping coffee. I stopped to talk with them about their ride, envious of their relaxed morning setup and cups full of hot coffee.

Back on the bike, I caught up to Sarah, who was refilling her water bottles. She looked relieved to have water again in this dry basin. The remaining thirty miles of dirt road riding was smooth sailing. A couple of horses crossed the road just in front of us, and I watched a few pronghorns effortlessly run through the desert-like grass, breaking the monotony of the barren scenery.

When the road turned to pavement, it became a nightmare. It wasn't the wind or a climb. No, it was just a flat road with a bad surface. Every twenty feet I hit a jolting crack in the pavement, preventing any kind of pedaling rhythm or comfortable spot in the saddle. It pounded me crack after crack after crack. To make matters worse, I could see the road stretching out for miles ahead, and I knew the beating would continue. After cursing the road, the intersection with Highway 287 finally came into view. Rawlins, and plenty of food options, were only few miles away. Along the jaw jarring paved section, I had gotten ahead of Sarah. She had an extremely tough time along that portion of pavement, as I found out when we ran into each other again at Brush Mountain Lodge.

Those few miles into Rawlins were actually long, hot miles through a major construction zone. The road was a single lane, and the cars traveling on 287 had to wait and follow a "pace" car through this stretch. The workers let me ride ahead of the pace car, giving me the chance to enjoy the newly laid asphalt surface without any cars passing. Those smooth blissful miles were in stark contrast to the previous jaw jarring road. The day was heating up, probably the hottest of the ride up to that point. I longed for a cold Coke and something other than a cheeseburger as I entered Rawlins.

The town gets a bad reputation among Tour Divide riders because of the volume of cars, occasional impolite drivers, and overall grungy look. I suspect it's because the riders were grumpy from having to first ride on that damn bumpy road and then a US highway getting into town. For me, I saw it as just another interstate town. Not bad, not good, but a town to rest and refuel. I stopped at the first gas station on the edge of town for that cold Coke. Then I went to a Chinese buffet where I could eat something for lunch that wasn't a bacon cheeseburger. The heat left me without a huge appetite, and I only managed a couple of plates of rice, noodles, chicken, and vegetables. A paltry amount considering all of the riding I had been doing over the last two weeks. The unquenchable hunger that so many Tour Divide riders developed never materialized for me. At least it kept the food bills lower.

Outside of the restaurant, I called my wife.

"I'm in Rawlins. Tomorrow I'll be in Colorado!" I said.

"We're excited that you are so close, but are you sure you still want us to meet you in Breckenridge when you get there?" she asked.

"Yes, I want to see you and the boys. Plus, my mom is flying out to meet me too."

"I'm just making sure you want to see us. A few people on the bikepacking.net forums are really making a big deal about race violations."

"What are you talking about?" I asked.

"I've been following the forums, and some of the guys on there are listening to the MTBCast call-ins, pointing out people's rule violations. I want to make sure that you really want to violate the rules and not officially place in the race. You worked really hard, and I don't want you to regret seeing us."

I asked her for more details about what they were saying. Basically, some people were dissecting the rider's call-ins, and flagging perceived race violations. While the Tour Divide is an underground race, it does have its own set of rules. The primary rule is that riders are not permitted to accept any kind of outside help, including from other riders. Put another way, if it's not something that each racer has access to, then you can't do it. Examples of violations include accepting water when you've run out, or staying inside a house while a thunderstorm drops torrents of rain outside.

"Yeah, those rules can get quite iffy. I've been really careful to not break any of the rules. But, seeing you is the one rule I'm willing to break. I'm going to be less than 100 miles away from home, and I really want to see you guys," I said.

"Are you sure? We all really want to see you, but we don't want you to break the rules if you're going to regret it later."

"I know it makes me an unofficial racer, but I want to see you, the boys, and my mom. This race has never been about my official ranking. It's always been a personal test," I said.

We continued to talk for a few more minutes. After hanging up the phone, I was fired up that people were dissecting call-ins and searching for rule violations, rather than encouraging the racers who gave everything they had day in and day out. I left Rawlins with an angry mind. For only the second time during the race, I turned on my iPod and cranked up Rage Against the Machine to match my fight-the-man mood. My pedals took the brunt of my frustration as I mashed on them while climbing south from Rawlins.

An hour outside of town, I came upon a huge construction project paving a twenty-mile stretch of dirt road. My timing was perfect as I hit this section at 5:00 p.m. when there was almost no work being done. Just lots of trucks making final runs and kicking up dust. During this section, I ran into a number of touring riders heading northbound. It was nice to stop and talk to them for a few minutes and hear about their journeys. Listening to their travels got me out of my mental funk and into a better mood to enjoy my ride once again.

When the sun began to set, I had ridden through all but the last mile or so of the construction zone. My shins were fatigued to the point where I had no power to ride up hills. I had a choice. I could either walk in the dark up the hills or camp for the night. My motivation to ride into the night and get me closer to Brush Mountain Lodge simply wasn't there. I set up camp for the night just before reaching Aspen Alley. I planned to see Aspen Alley in the early morning light, and then enjoy a hot breakfast and some coffee after riding the forty miles to Brush Mountain Lodge - my fist stop back in my home state of Colorado.

The next morning, I packed up camp and started riding soon after the sunrise, allowing me to catch some nice pictures of Aspen Alley as the sun filtered through the trees. Unfortunately, the construction work had removed quite a few of the aspens, leaving it a little less picturesque than previous years. Even so, my fourteenth day of riding was off to a good start.

Soon after Aspen Alley, I reached a section of pavement with a fast downhill that took me to the Colorado border. A left turn crossed the Little Snake River and began the dirt road climb up to Brush Mountain Lodge. I looked forward to meeting Kirsten who runs Brush Mountain, ready to drink some coffee while listening to her stories.

The dirt climb was ten miles long. The first mile or two followed the river, passing by several houses in a comfortable climb. Then my energy left me. I had nothing left. My pace dropped to a crawl, and I walked anywhere the grade steepened. Two days with minimum caffeine (and zero coffee since Pinedale before the Basin) was taking its toll. I kept repeating to myself, "Just get to the Lodge." If anyone saw my blue dot on Trackleaders at the time, I'm sure they wondered how a rider could move that slow. A caterpillar moved faster than me during those long, slow miles.

When I finally turned the corner and saw Brush Mountain Lodge to the left, my spirits instantly lifted. Brush Mountain meant food, coffee, and a giant welcoming hug from Kirsten. I sat down on the porch with a large cup of coffee, the caffeine slowing bringing life back into me. Kirsten made a breakfast of pancakes, sausage, and a giant bowl of cherries, and followed that up with another round of food. I probably had six cups of coffee to go with all of the food.

Sarah Caylor arrived as I ate my breakfast. Our conversation turned to the bikepacking.net forums and how this year seemed to have the most issues with riders not following the "rules," as well as people critiquing the riders on the forums.

I felt like the forum posters should be supporting the riders through such a brutal race, especially with the weather we encountered during the first week. There is a time and place for talking about rules and making changes. During the race is not one of them. Kirsten had a few comments and then came out with a simple and profound statement.

"Ignore the phone and ride your bike. It's your race, you know the rules, and you don't need forum posters to validate or invalidate what you are doing out on the route."

Ignore your phone and ride your bike.

Even though the food was physically what I needed, talking with Kirsten and the two guys helping her around the ranch was, by far, the best part. It was nice to sit, relax, and talk to people. Plus, Kirsten's perspective on the race rejuvenated me.

20

Hospitality

T HE HUG. The happiness, the care, the kindness that was wrapped up in that giant hug Kirsten gave me that morning. Every rider was greeted with that same type of hug and a huge smile when they made it to Brush Mountain Lodge, regardless of the time.

Kirsten watches the SPOT tracker of riders, estimating when they will arrive. As it gets late into the night, she watches to see if they will camp on the side of the road or keep pushing. The hospitality and friendliness make Brush Mountain Lodge one of the must-stop places on the Tour Divide route.

Just like Ovando, Montana, and Pie Town, New Mexico, riders over the years have had their spirits lifted and in some cases, races rejuvenated by the kindness that pours out of Brush Mountain Lodge. From a glance at a map, they don't look any different than the other lodging and food options. In person, they are places that transform bad days into good days, and good days into incredible days.

In all three places, there is one person that is well known for taking care of riders.

In Ovando, it's Angler.

In Pie Town, it's Nita.

At Brush Mountain, it's Kirsten.

Unlike the towns of Ovando and Pie Town that have other residents and business to support the riders, at Brush Mountain there is only Kirsten. No other buildings or restaurants or people. She manages to take care of all of the riders with her amazing hospitality mixed with a healthy dose of reality. I don't know how she manages to stay so upbeat and energetic after having racers come in at all times of the day and night.

As I struggled my way up the mountain that morning, I was so thankful that she was there, waiting for my slow moving SPOT dot to arrive. My attitude was instantly transformed from one of hurt and self-pity to one of optimism and happiness. It was all thanks to Kirsten and her immense kindness that flows out towards everyone she meets.

Why would someone open up their lodge to cyclists who have been out on the trail for almost two weeks? Let's face it, we are dirty, smelly, and craving plates full of food.

It takes a special kind of person.

Why would someone stay up until the early hours of the morning just to make sure a rider has a warm bed and a full stomach?

It takes a special kind of person.

It's not for money, or for fame, or for any other reason than being nice to other people. She simply wants to create a bright spot for them. And what a bright spot it is. For every racer, whether first place or last place, Kirsten is waiting there ready to greet them with a hug and provide anything they need. There are no invoices or prices posted. It's all done out of kindness towards the riders.

A Dream Worth Living

While the kindness on display at Brush Mountain Lodge was extraordinary and over the top, almost every day of the race had brought some form of hospitality and kindness. From Rocky in Elkford offering to let us stay at his gym, to the town of Ovando rolling out the welcome mat and posting notes from the rider's families and friends, to the anonymous person in Helena whose front yard contained the table full of snacks. (Oh, those mangoes!) Sometimes, it was the simple curiosity of a customer at a gas station in Rawlins, Wyoming, when they said hello and asked a few questions about the bike, the route, and the amount of food that I could stuff into a frame bag. There is hope for humanity. I saw it in the smiling faces that greeted me throughout the race - the vicious wild dogs in New Mexico excluded.

A giant hug greeted me when I arrived at Brush Mountain. My farewell warranted another hug. I rode away, extremely grateful for Kirsten and how she treated all of us during the race.

21

The Mountain Lion

WITH THAT FINAL GIANT HUG from Kirsten and two PB&J sandwiches for the road, I left Brush Mountain Lodge feeling like I could conquer the world. Food and people can really change your attitude. To make the morning even better, the scenery after Brush Mountain Lodge was much nicer than the Aspen Alley view. At least, it was in my opinion.

The rest of the morning was typical of the Tour Divide - lonely dirt roads, climbing, rocks, and descending. The last descent before arriving at the Clark Store was really rough. There were many big rocks in the road. Rocks that happened to be the same color as the dirt, so I didn't see the rock until I practically ran into it. I guess I could have gone slower and been more careful. But where is the fun in that?

The Clark Store had sandwiches, snacks, and most importantly, ice cream! I had ridden from Canada to Colorado, 1400 miles, without having any ice cream. Coffee and ice cream are usually my go-to food groups. It was time to make sure those food groups received a little more attention.

After my much-needed ice cream, I continued riding. I wanted to make it past Steamboat Springs, Colorado in order to ride into Breckenridge to meet my family the following day. Up to this point, through all of the rain, snow, mud, and dust, my bike had only needed new front brake pads in Butte, Montana. In Steamboat, I stopped at Orange Peel Bikes to get new tire sealant and rear brake pads. While in town, I also got a burrito to go and a box of instant coffee. From now on, no matter where I slept, I would have my all-important coffee.

I rode on the bike paths, and a few miles later was on the outskirts of town. The sun started to set as I stopped on the side of the dirt road to eat my burrito and take a short break before the long climb up Lynx Pass. I wanted to ride as far as I could, but I knew this would be my last climb of the day, based on how my ankle and shin had been hurting as I rode. I hoped to finish with a 115 mile day, leaving another 115 miles to Breckenridge.

The route passed through Stagecoach State Park, and then followed a short stretch of singletrack surrounded by a small lake and several houses. The last pale light of the day vanished as I meandered around the lake. Once I exited the singletrack on the other side of the lake, the climb up Lynx Pass started in earnest. Darkness settled in as the road took me higher and higher into the mountains. At first, there were numerous houses on either side of the road. Slowly, fewer driveways appeared, and fewer lights could be seen through the trees.

The road and surrounding mountains shrank into my own little world, illuminated by the beam from my dynamo powered headlight. As long as I pedaled, the world had a diameter of thirty feet. Beyond that boundary, I could distinguish the road from the grass lining it, or the trees from the road, but not much else. Was there a cliff on one side? How far did the mountains stretch out before me? Those were questions that I could not answer. The babbling sound of water running in a small creek just to the right of the road was audible. The only other sound was that of my breathing and my tires rolling through the dirt and pebbles of the road.

It was the peacefulness of night riding at its finest. 10:00 p.m. with a bike, a rider, a small light, and darkness surrounding them on all sides.

Off to my right, along the creek, a rustling sound interrupted my moment of peacefulness. Suddenly, a mountain lion darted out of the brush and ran across the road not more than twenty feet in front of me. My light beam held the mountain lion in perfect view as it ran from my right to my left and then up into the steep hillside. Time seemed to stand still for the split second it took for the lion to cross the road. My first reaction was, "Oh cool, a mountain lion," which was quickly replaced with "Oh s#!t, a mountain lion!"

The cat didn't look at me as it ran across the road. Maybe it was my lights that scared it away from the creek or the sound of the tires on the dirt. Regardless of the reason, I wasn't interested in discussing them with the mountain lion. As I pedaled, I quickly turned on my helmet light and used its faint beam to scan the rocky hillside to my left.

Where is the mountain lion?
Did it keep running?
Can I see any eyes in my headlight beam?
Does bear spray work on a mountain lion?

163

I found no sign of eyes peering back at me. I heard no growl or hissing, just the sound of my tires in the quiet night.

With a huge shot of adrenaline coursing through my veins, my tired legs suddenly sparked to life. My pedal cadence increased, spinning me up the hill at a pace not attainable earlier in the climb. With a mountain lion somewhere nearby, power was much easier to find. Funny how that works.

After the initial rush of emotions (mostly scared, but also excited) and riding quickly up the road, my thoughts turned to camping for the night. Prior to the mountain lion incident, I had been keeping an eye out for a camping spot. It was late and the 115 miles of mountain riding had tired me out. In my head, a debate waged about whether or not I should stop for the night. It had only been a mile or two since I saw the mountain lion, which meant it could still be close by. My brain told me to keep riding for at least thirty more minutes to put distance between me and the cat. But I was tired, and my fear lost out to stopping and sleeping for the night.

The "perfect" camping spot soon appeared, a flat grassy area next to a split-rail fence. It was the entrance to some sort of private ranch or hunting club. I reasoned that if I placed the entrance to my tarp against the fence, I'd have protection against the mountain lion if it returned. Well, not really protection in the real sense of the word, but it made me feel better with something on all sides. Just in case the lion was around, I hung my food away from my campsite. With the warmth of my down quilt surrounding me, my breathing slowed, and I tried to push thoughts of mountain lions out of my head.

22

Solo Camping

FOR ALMOST EVERY RIDER, THE Tour Divide experience involves times where you are utterly alone. Nothing but a little blip with two rolling tires in a big, giant world.

During the day, these times are generally enjoyable. Ok, maybe when I saw the sign announcing grizzly bears in the area on Union Pass in Wyoming, it was a little unnerving to be out there on my own. Most of the time, the solo riding gave me a chance to keep my own schedule, think about whatever was on my mind, and talk to myself without any strange looks from others.

Once the sun went behind the mountains to be replaced with stars and a moon, the feeling of being alone became harder to accept. Uneasiness and fear replaced the comfort from the daylight hours. The prospect of spending a night out in the woods completely alone was not one familiar to me.

In fact, solo camping was my greatest fear heading into the race. It even outweighed my concern over bears. And now here I was, searching for a camping spot after have just seen a mountain lion.

Had this encounter happened during the first few days of the race, I'm fairly certain I would have kept riding. That mountain lion would have consumed my thoughts. Stopping for the night within a few miles of the sighting would have been impossible.

By the time I arrived in Colorado, I had camped by myself a total of two times on the Tour Divide - outside of Lima, Montana and the night near Aspen Alley. Add in the first time I went bikepacking, for a total of three nights I had spent alone in the woods.

How had solo camping changed from a nerve-wracking experience to an evening I looked forward to? I think the answer lies in how we conquer other challenges in our lives. Remember that first day of high school? I arrived in a knot of nerves, worry, and anxiousness. By the time the second or third day rolled around, comfort started to settle in.

Or what about taking a newborn home as a first-time parent? It was both exhausting and scary for me. After a few diaper changes and naps - ok, maybe more like two or three days of that - I realized that I could actually make it work.

Or think about the first time diving into the deep-end of the pool? My dad was in the pool waiting to catch me. Still, the fear gripped me, holding my feet tight against the edge. Finally, I pushed away the fear and made the leap, my dad catching me with a smile on his face. After that moment, my parents couldn't drag me out of the deep-end that seemed so terrifying moments earlier.

Camping is no different. The first solo night is terrifying. I know it was for me, on my first bikepacking trip. The process of eating dinner after setting up camp was easy enough. However, making the move to crawl into my sleeping bag and close my eyes for sleep felt like it would take more strength than I had. I felt like I was at the edge of a moat, teeming with snakes and crocodiles and piranhas, while also being too wide for me to jump across. Make a wrong move and I would find the sharp end of many teeth.

As the night darkened and time ticked by, I convinced myself that the feelings were just that - feelings. After I took one last look and made sure there were no animals around, I got into my sleeping bag and zipped up my tent door. It was a big step, but only the first one.

I endured hours of feeling like every sound I heard was an animal coming to get me. Happy thoughts, just a few happy thoughts were all that I wanted. Eventually, through all of the tricks my mind played with the sounds, I drifted off to a light sleep for a few hours.

Awakening the following morning when the sunlight hit the tent, I realized what I had accomplished. Something that seemed impossible before became very real. I turned into a solo camper. Easy? No. Overcoming a fear is not supposed to be easy. It is, however, something that brings accomplishment and pride.

On my first solo night of the Tour Divide, there was still nervousness, doubt, and a small amount of fear as I settled into my down quilt and closed my eyes to the world. Finally, on my third night of solo camping, I was able to lay down and close my eyes without fear being one of my primary feelings.

With each new sunrise that greeted my eyes and my solitary campsite, the prospect of sleeping alone in the woods at night became more enjoyable.

23

Limping into Breckenridge

O N THE SLOPES OF LYNX PASS, there were no "visitors" during the night. Or if there were, I was deep asleep and did not notice.

Upon waking, I packed up my camp and continued climbing up the mountain. About thirty minutes into riding, I started to warm up, so I decided to stop for breakfast. What do you do when you have candy bars, one PB&J sandwich, and an instant coffee packet? Well, I made a PB&J&C sandwich - sprinkle the coffee granules on the inside of the sandwich and you get instant breakfast and coffee. "Bitter" and "unpleasant" are the words that describe the taste. Even though it was not my finest coffee moment, it got the job done and fueled me for more riding.

The downhill after Lynx Pass crossed a paved highway and then brought me to a crossing of Rock Creek. It wasn't a tiny creek crossing, but looked quite deep and wide. Deep enough that I didn't want to simply plow through it to reach the other side. I walked back and forth along the creek, trying to find a shallow place to cross. There were no better options. I tried to ride through the main channel, but ended up putting my feet down and walking the last few feet. If I wasn't fully awake before the crossing, I certainly was afterwards.

Where there's a creek crossing, a climb always follows. The next climb was not too bad, but the downhill was excruciatingly painful. Not because of it being rough or technical; it simply wouldn't go downhill. There would be the tease of a half-mile downhill section that was followed by a quarter-mile climb so steep I was forced to walk. The short downhill followed by steep climbing happened over and over, putting extra strain on my already-sore ankles. Finally, the views opened up and the route went down to the Colorado River.

Climbing up from the river was steep and hot. The grade remained steep as the dirt turned to pavement. I caught up to Brian Bridau on this climb and we chatted for a bit before the steepness of the climb split us up. As soon as the downhill started, I flew towards Kremmling. Tucked into the aero bars and reaching speeds in excess of 40 mph always puts a smile on my face.

I decided against taking the detour into Kremmling because I had plenty of food and water to reach Breckenridge. I was on a mission to see my family. I stopped on the side of the road for a lunch break, giving my ankles a rest before the final push to Silverthorne and then Breckenridge.

Ute Pass was the last big climb of the day. The dirt section of the climb was enjoyable as it climbed alongside a river and a few campgrounds.

"Thank goodness I'm on dirt," I said to myself. Up ahead, a paved road rose steeply up the mountain. Several miles later, my dirt road turned into pavement and I was ascending that steep paved road. The climbing hurt...a lot. I was left walking up a paved road again, and my ankles were reaching their breaking point. Each day, my shin and Achilles "gave out" after a certain amount of miles. Some days the limit was 100 miles. Other days, it was 150 miles. After they "gave out", I found it very difficult to ride any further. I reached my daily limit on Ute Pass, but I still needed to ride thirty miles before I got to Breckenridge.

Riding down from Ute Pass to Highway 9 was rip-roaring descent on pavement. A chilly, light rain started to fall, but I remained tucked into the aero bars, riding as fast as possible. The highway into Silverthorne had a wide shoulder, and the ride was fairly flat. However, my shin and Achilles had been through enough for the day, and no longer wanted to cooperate, making for several unpleasant miles.

When I rolled into Silverthorne and stopped at a gas station, I didn't want to ride into Breckenridge. At that moment, the gas station had a couple of tables inside that were a lot more comfortable than my bike. Had my family not been waiting for me in Breckenridge, I may have called it a day, stayed longer in Silverthorne to rest. Instead, I lingered a few extra minutes before I packed up my gear and headed out of town on the bike path, ready to meet my family.

The path climbs up a set of switchbacks on the way up to a dam. I ran into another cyclist on the path as he was riding up to his apartment. He recognized me as a Divide racer and we chatted about the trip on our way up the climb. It's these kinds of random moments and people that make this ride something special. Ten minutes earlier, I was down in the dumps mentally. After meeting one other cyclist and chatting for short time, I was feeling much better and excited to be riding.

It was 7:00 p.m. when I made it to Breckenridge. I rode up to the hotel and headed to the outdoor pool. I could hear laughter and splashing as I got close. Opening the pool gate, I saw my two boys playing in the water, a very welcome sight for my sore eyes.

I knew going into Breckenridge that meeting my family there violated one of the rules of the Tour Divide. I made the decision to see them even though I would have to relegate myself from the official placings.

Looking back now that I have finished, I would make the same decision again without any hesitation.

24

Rules Matter.
Until They Don't.

THIS CHAPTER IS DIRECTED TOWARDS *my kids, but it's also a manifesto for anyone that's a dreamer, a creative, or struggling to find themselves. Keep on pushing the limits and the boundaries that people try to construct around you.*

Life has an interesting way of making you aware of what truly matters.

Throughout Canada, Montana, and Wyoming, I rode through spectacular scenery. These were areas I dreamed about riding through, and I was finally making that dream a reality. My heart tingled each time I crested a mountain pass and looked out at the beauty in front of me.

But every time I talked to you on the phone during the first week of the race, I couldn't say two words without crying. Your voice on the other end tugged at my heart even more than the race. Tears welled up in my eyes. Every. Single. Time.

So, that's why it was such an easy decision for me to break the Tour Divide rules when I hobbled up to hug you, mom, and grandma in Breckenridge. I was simply following my heart, letting my soul speak to me. Sure, the Tour Divide was very important to me. I dedicated almost a year of training to my preparation. But it was not my top priority. The feelings triggered by talking to you during the race confirmed what truly, deeply mattered to me more than anything else - my family.

Nothing will ever change that. Nothing will ever compare to the feeling of holding you for the first time. Not a job, not a race result, not any amount of money. Nothing. On the day you were born, my heart smiled and my soul shined brighter than ever before.

You don't find your "one thing" by listening to an expert or following popular trends. No, it comes from deep within you, and it may take some time to figure out. When you do find "it", you'll feel the spark inside your heart when you think about "it," or share a room with "them," or work on "it."

I first noticed it when riding motorcycles and mountain bikes in the woods. Then again when I discovered my brain was wired to program computers. And then like an electric shock when I fell in love with your mom.

When your soul sings, you know what truly matters to you. Nothing else is important. Not even the rules of something you spent months or years working towards. Did you ever think you would hear your dad say that? I'll let you in on a secret about rules.

They matter...until they don't.

Stopping at red lights matters. Being honest matters. Someone preventing you from playing a sport because of your size doesn't matter. Rules against wearing certain colors together don't matter (you've already figured this one out based on the crazy outfits you wear to school). Rules that force you to live against your priorities don't matter.

Rules are necessary. Silly rules not so much. And stupid rules have no place but the trash can (Examples: the one requiring field hockey players to use a right-handed stick, or any that prevent you from loving whoever you love).

If you are ever faced with a choice where rules and your feelings are not in agreement, always choose based on the feelings that are core to you. Be true to yourself. Never make a choice because you have to follow someone else's rules, because you don't.

Remember when we watched the movie Rudy? He wanted nothing more than to play football at Notre Dame. Of course he wasn't big enough, or fast enough. His grades weren't good enough. The rules said he couldn't get into the school and he certainly couldn't play football for one of the top teams in the nation. Instead of giving up, he tried harder than he had ever tried. He pushed his limits and other people's limits too. The rules were not going to stop him from making his dream a reality.

When you find what you enjoy most, what you love, who you love, go for it with everything you have.

"You've got this!"

There will be naysayers. Ignore them.

There will be doubts in your mind. Push through them.

There will be pain and suffering. That's ok. It will make the goal even more meaningful when you arrive.

If you have to break some rules along the way, that's ok as long as you are being honest and following your heart.

Following the rules is easy and boring. Following the tug of the beliefs and values wrapped around the core of your soul pays off in the most amazing ways. The heavens and earth align, creating a perfect moment where time slows down. You'll feel every motion, every sound, every thought running through your mind. The numbers and letters on a page look like they are floating into the right configuration. The pedal strokes on a bike are effortless as you take a turn and feel the connection between yourself, the bike, and the dirt. The world fades away as you lose yourself in the perfect loving eyes of your true love.

Keep pushing until you find those feelings.

Don't let anything stand in your way. If it's starting your own business, or traveling the world, or being a dad, or something that doesn't yet exist, go for it! (Now, if it's bike touring, please call your dad and invite him because I'd love to tag along.)

Regardless of the what you do, always be true to yourself. Use the spark inside you as a guide.

Who you are is so much more important than what you do or how you do it.

PART THREE

Drive

Life is like a ten speed bicycle. Most of us have gears we never use.

— CHARLES M. SCHULZ

25

A Tipi by the Creek

W HEN I ARRIVED IN BRECKENRIDGE, the soreness in my ankle made even walking difficult. It hurt to move. At the same time, it felt wonderful to hug my boys and give my wife a long overdue kiss.

They all greeted me and then proceeded to tell me how much I stunk! For four nights, I camped on the side of the road and pedaled all day to reach Breckenridge. My skin was barely visible under the layer upon layer of sweat, dust, and sunscreen. Earlier in the day, I came to realize how bad I smelled. While riding on a lonely road, I caught a whiff of foul odor. There were no dead animals on the road, no other riders around, and no houses to be seen. I smelled that bad.

I cleaned up as best I could and iced my ankles while my kids told me about their experiences over the last two weeks while I had been racing - their days at Vacation Bible School, the ways they were helping at home, and the fun they were having with grandma, who had flown out from South Carolina.

Over dinners of pasta and ravioli, we talked more about their time away from dad. I described the feeling of riding into Ovando, the awesome breakfast at Brush Mountain Lodge, my first solo camping night in Montana, and of course the mountain lion encounter.

Hearing their voices made me smile. Holding my wife's hand while walking back from dinner was soothing. After two weeks of struggle, my family gave me comfort and allowed me to relax ever so slightly. I knew I had to leave the following day, but the few hours we spent together made me realize how much support they provided, as well as how much of a burden they shouldered with me being gone so long.

It's easy to think the riding, day after day, is the hard part of the race without thinking about those back home. They endure a different kind of struggle, but one that is equally challenging - the worry about their loved one, the disruption to routines, and all household burdens dumped onto them.

The next day, my ankle felt better, but not by much. At the insistence of my wife and mom, I visited an Urgent Care facility. The doctor's advice was to rest my ankles for a few days. I planned to follow his advice - right after I reached the Mexico border. There were still over 1000 miles left to ride. Enduring the pain and adjusting to the fact that my ankle had a certain number of miles in it each day was the only way I could finish. I purchased KT tape from a running store in town. The store showed me the proper way to tape my Achilles and offered some ideas on how to tape my shin. I found the tape made a big difference.

With tape in place, I had time for one last meal with my family before they went back home. It turns out that seeing your family in the middle of a three week race is not as easy as it sounds. While I loved seeing them, eating meals with them, and talking with them, it was excruciatingly difficult to say goodbye to them again. After lunch, we lingered over ice cream before I finally said goodbye. Although it wasn't the sob-fest like leaving them at the Denver airport before the race, it was another difficult goodbye with plenty of tears. The mental boost from seeing my wife and kids was equally offset by the heartbreak of saying goodbye for at least another week.

At 3:00 p.m., my eyes obscured by tears, I rode down Main Street towards Boreas Pass, taking one last look back at my family waving from the sidewalk. Being so late in the day, I decided to ride no farther than the fifty miles to Hartsel. It was a limit rather than a goal - based on the hope that another short day would help my body heal.

Just before the turn to go up Boreas Pass, I ran into Kent McDonald and Patrick Day. Kent was riding the Tour Divide after having recently retired. Pat was a soft spoken rider who pedaled without many words. Having riding companions up the gentle climb, probably the most enjoyable climb on the Tour Divide route, was a blessing in several ways. It was nice to have some companions after riding solo for a number of days, and talking with other riders meant I didn't focus as much on leaving my family behind.

Coming down Boreas Pass, I got ahead of Kent and Pat as I turned onto the Gold Dust Trail. It's a fun trail with banked turns that would be even more fun on an unloaded bike. I enjoyed the short trail ride and was back on the gravel road headed for Como. At the bottom of the climb, I stopped to take some pictures of the now wide open expanse of South Park, Colorado. A woman driving in the opposite direction stopped to take my picture. We proceeded to chat for ten minutes about the ride and her journeys into the mountains even though she was fighting heart and breathing issues. It was another of those moments on the ride where a simple interaction with a complete stranger lifts yours spirits.

The road from Como to Hartsel is flat-ish and fast when there are favorable winds. The area around South Park is always windy, and on this day a tailwind blew from north to south. Kent came flying by me tucked in his aero bars followed soon after by Pat with both of them smiling, whooping, and enjoying the tailwind. I managed to keep close to them thanks to a few uphill, non-aero sections. The three of us rode into Hartsel for a meal at the Highline Café. Of course it was another excellent burger, supplemented this time with pie and ice cream. Two servings of ice cream in one day. That's a much better ratio of days on the road to ice cream helpings.

Boy, I was wiped out after my whopper of a fifty mile day. Not exactly, but I wasn't going to ride any further. I had pushed the limit the day before, and I knew I needed the rest. Kent and Pat finished their milkshakes and rode off at dusk to take advantage of the favorable tailwind before it had a chance to shift, leaving me alone at the table.

"Is there anywhere I could camp around town? Maybe the church or somewhere?" I asked the waitress.

"No, not really. And tomorrow is Sunday so the church is not a good idea."

"True. Hmmm......" I replied, trailing off with a look of dejection in my eyes.

"I'll tell you what. Stay here and let me go check in the bar. I'll be right back."

Maybe it was the look in my eyes or simply another stranger being nice. A couple of minutes later, she walked back and said, "I've got a plan for you."

I camped across the road on some land that one of the bar patrons owned. As long as I stayed quiet and concealed, it wouldn't be a problem. There was no argument from me and I thanked her several times. Not only did I have a place to camp, I was also close to the cafe, which meant I could enjoy a full-sized breakfast the following morning. Perfect!

I set up camp and laid down with the sounds of a Saturday night at the bar in the background. As I was settling in to sleep, Scotty came over and setup camp next to me. I first met Scotty while hiking through the snow on Red Meadow Pass. We then crossed paths again in Lima, MT at Jan's Cafe. I was happy to see him again.

"Hey Andy, nice to see you."

"Good to see you too. Guess you ate at the café and asked about camping?"

"She told me you were already setup over here. She was very nice."

"Definitely. See you in the morning for breakfast."

In the morning, we walked over to the café for our breakfast, and what a delicious breakfast it was. Of course, when I saw biscuits and gravy on the menu, I was sold. I talked up my favorite breakfast so much, Scotty decided to go with a half order for himself. He had never heard of biscuits and gravy, but they must have been good since he finished the entire plate.

Full of food and coffee, we headed off towards Salida in the chilly morning air. It was a beautiful clear morning with bright blue skies all around us. The route even passed by a sign pointing towards Guffey, Colorado, where my wife's family used to raise cattle. This was going to be a good day.

Wide and smooth dirt roads without many climbs were laid out before us as we discussed riding, life, and our families. His wife was meeting him after the race to spend some time sightseeing around the western United States. As the morning continued, we talked about lifestyle differences between New Zealand and the U.S. as well as differences on how citizens in each country perceived camping on their land. Let's just say that New Zealand sounds like a great place to go for some bikepacking. Scotty's attitude towards everything was relaxed and easy going, something I wish I could do more of. The miles rolled by almost effortlessly as we talked and took in the open scenery with brilliant blue skies overhead. This section felt very similar to the peaceful and calm ride outside of Pinedale with the Wind River range in the distance.

The only snag was the one big climb before Salida. Since our climbing speeds were different, the long climb took me back into solo riding mode. Towards the top, the road steepened and I found myself walking again. I knew at this point to take it easy whenever possible so my ankle would hold up better. The KT tape I applied in Breckenridge helped, or at least gave me the illusion of helping. Either way, my ankle felt better.

The downhill into Salida came with built-in brakes in the form of a very stiff headwind. If I stopped pedaling, I slowed down enough to navigate the tightest of turns without touching the brakes. Personally, I'd rather be bombing down the hill and using plenty of brakes.

In Salida, I stopped at Absolute Bikes for a quick drivetrain cleaning and new tire sealant. While the excellent crew there worked on the bike, I went next door for a quick meal, this time skipping the burger and opting for a tasty pulled pork sandwich with sweet potato fries. Scotty arrived as I ate my lunch, and we rode out of town together.

The same wind that provided brakes on the downhill into Salida was now hitting us like a blast furnace cranked up to high. The combination of the temperature, the hot wind, and riding on asphalt made for a tough ride leaving town. Compounding the misery, we rode on the shoulder of Highway 285 with its trucks and RVs zooming past. The right turn onto the dirt road leading up Marshall Pass was a welcomed sight, even though it led to fifteen more miles of climbing. After two weeks out on the ride, a dirt road without traffic, even if it was part of a 3000 foot climb was preferred over cars and a town. It felt better to be out on the quiet roads with the trees, the dust, and an animal or two.

The weather was cooler, the skies were still an amazing blue, and the climb towards the top was enjoyable. The views of the mountains against the brilliant blue sky were stunning. As I soaked in the scenery, it got even better. O'Haver Lake came into view as the road climbed around and above the lake, revealing one of those pictures you would expect to see on a postcard - a clear mountain lake, pine trees, and blue skies at 9,000 feet.

At the top, the Continental Divide Trail, the Colorado Trail, and the Tour Divide route all connect. A trifecta of trails that could one day bring me back to that point in time was interesting to think about as I ate a snack and took a few pictures. Then it was back to reality to make sure I finished the Tour Divide before dreaming of other rides and hikes.

The sun started to set as I pedaled my way down the mountain. It made for some more great pictures as the sun's highlights bathed the grassy meadows and the hillsides in soft golden hues. The maps indicated Sargents and Highway 50 at the bottom of the climb. According to the ACA maps, all services were available in Sargents, so I expected a town. What I found instead was one store that contained all services - gas station, restaurant, hotel, camping, and grocery store. It's funny how you read the map and expect one thing in your mind. The reality is usually much different. Not that it really mattered because they had hot food and a place to stay, which is all I really needed.

Upon walking into the main building, I was welcomed with a friendly greeting. Laid out before me was one short aisle of candy, snacks, and drinks with a handful of restaurant tables on the other side of the room. At the counter, I inquired about my camping options for the night. It turned out, not only did they have a campground, but also cabins and tipis were available. I had planned to set up my tarp in the campground, but once I heard the word tipi, my decision was made, and I sat down for dinner.

With a salad and yet another burger ordered, I asked about breakfast options for the morning. (Of course, I was going to ask about breakfast and coffee!) Unfortunately, the restaurant didn't open until 8:00 a.m. which was too late for my planned departure. I moved to Plan B - get my coffee fix from whatever drinks they had in the "grocery" section. A few short steps brought be back over to the grocery aisle where orange juice, cold Starbucks coffee, cashews, and more candy bars found their way into my arms.

I obtained a tipi, warm dinner, morning coffee, and gas station food for the next several meals within a fifty foot radius. Not bad, not bad.

I would be sleeping in a tipi, a first for me. While unpacking my air mattress and down quilt, I saw Scotty reach the bottom of the downhill and stop in front of the store.

"Hey Scotty, over here!", I yelled as I walked back towards the store.

"That was a fun downhill," he said with a smile still on his face.

"Yeah. I was going to camp, but they had tipis. So I couldn't pass that up."

"A tipi?"

"Sounded like an interesting place to camp to me. It's just behind the store. You're welcome to share the tipi with me," I added.

"Ok, let me get some food. I hope they are still open," he said.

Scotty managed to get a meal and snacks minutes before the store closed for the night.

Overall, it had been a really good day, even though my mileage was less than 100 miles. I had a new friendship, and saw some amazing Colorado scenery.

The tipi sat ten feet away from Marshall Creek. The white canvas painted with bright blue, yellow, and red designs stood in stark contrast to our bikes outfitted with black bikepacking gear and a two-week layer of mud and dirt. Inside, the tipi contained enough room to sleep four comfortably. Electric and propane hookups were a modern twist on the otherwise rustic feel of the accommodations. Scotty and I took advantage of the floor space, spreading out gear, food, and clothing as we organized for the next day. Being able to stand and move around made these activities much easier. Usually, I performed these activities under my tiny tarp that barely covered me, sitting hunched over a small amount of gear.

Darkness and the cool night air descended on Sargents as we talked about Scotty's firsts for the day - biscuits and gravy, the stunning bright blue Colorado skies, and staying in a tipi.

"You're becoming a full-fledged American. All you need is a cowboy hat."

"No, I need a Dodge Ram truck," he replied with his dry sense of humor.

"Good point," I said, while laughing at his quick reply.

A hot meal, plenty of food for the following day, the company of a new friend, and a creek babbling next to a tipi is a fantastic way to end any day.

26

Towns

BEING SURPRISED WHEN A TOWN is smaller than expected is actually a positive on the Tour Divide. The race makes you appreciate these smaller towns and outposts more than the larger ones. Why? It's easy to find everything you need in a single store or along a one-road town.

The tradeoff is that the smallest of the small have limited hours and food options. As the ride progressed, being picky about what to eat was never a problem. As long as it looked or smelled like food, I ate it. The issue became the luck of hitting the stores during their limited hours of operation. Early on, it was easier to skip a small outpost and wait until the next town to re-supply. Deeper into the route, skipping any type of re-supply became a huge gamble because options were spaced much further apart.

Even though my speed and progress was never quite as fast as my goals, I was very lucky in my timing for food and stores. Not once did I encounter a store that had closed a few minutes prior to my arrival like other riders experienced in places like Sargents, Ovando, or Hartsel. Even in Atlantic City with it's odd hours and closures, I managed to walk into the bar and enjoy a burger and fries in the early afternoon. Other riders arrived in Atlantic City only to find everything closed, forcing them to wait overnight in order to eat and restock before the long Great Basin journey.

I hit a few snags that changed my plans. In Eureka, the cafe was closed so I grabbed something for breakfast at the gas station across the street. In Hartsel, I slept in an extra hour, waiting for the restaurant to open at 7:00 a.m. Neither of these was a real inconvenience. In Hartsel, I could have easily gotten up early and ridden to Salida on the food reserves that were packed in my frame bag. By delaying my departure an hour, I ate a delicious breakfast and drank my fill of coffee.

On the other end of the spectrum are the larger towns along the route, with populations of more than 10,000 people. Bigger towns have a wide variety of re-supply options, such as Butte, Montana; Helena, Montana; Rawlins, Wyoming; and Silver City, New Mexico. The additional options make the town more difficult for a cyclist to navigate. Which road contains the stores or restaurants a rider so deeply depends on? Driving through a city in a car looking for a restaurant is no big deal. However, on a bike after a long day of riding, the last thing I wanted to do was pedal around town in circles trying to locate food and supplies.

The majority of towns along the Tour Divide fall somewhere in between the tiny outposts and larger towns. They are small towns with a full set of amenities for a traveling cyclist - restaurant, gas station, grocery, and hotel. A few of these small towns have the perfect layout. Places like Lincoln, Montana or Cuba, New Mexico have one main road with the gas station on one side, the restaurant on the other side, and the hotel at the far end of the street. In Tour Divide terms, it's an oasis. No wasted pedal strokes. No wasted energy. Even Goldilocks would be happy in these towns because they are not too big, and not too small, but just right.

Picking a favorite town is impossible because there were so many great little towns that provided the right service at the right time. Usually that was in the form of a bacon cheeseburger when I began to tire of the candy bars and cashews I carried on my bike.

As a Tour Divide rider, Helena, Montana proved to be the most challenging, due to its size. With that being said, I should state that there is nothing wrong with the town itself. I wasn't familiar with Helena, and found myself pedaling aimlessly around town, attempting to locate a hotel and restaurant. I was ready to relax, not increase my pedal strokes. The next morning, I couldn't find an open store for my morning coffee on the way out of town. Other riders may have had better luck navigating through Helena, but I learned the value of a smaller town.

(Note: For the purpose of these awards, a town is a location that contains a restaurant, grocery items, a gas station, and a hotel/cabin/campground. An outpost is a location that's smaller than a town and does not contain the full set of amenities.)

Town Awards

BIGGEST TOWN
Butte, Montana with a population of 34,000

SMALLEST TOWN
Sargents, Colorado with a population of 136

UNFRIENDLIEST TOWN

None. Everyone I met along the route was encouraging and greeted me with a smile.

Outpost Awards

It's impossible to name a best outpost because there were so many wonderful places. Here are some highlights from the people I met.

BEST HUG

Kirsten at Brush Mountain Lodge in Colorado. Not only do you get a greeting hug, you get a giant goodbye hug as well.

BEST GRANDFATHER

Squirrel Creek Ranch in Idaho. I never got his name, and I never interacted with another grandfather during the race. But when you open up on a Sunday morning and offer to make me a pot of coffee and a tasty breakfast, you have a special place in my heart.

BEST CONVERSATION

Cañon Plaza snack shack in New Mexico. Silvia invited me to sit inside, and we talked for about twenty minutes while I recharged with a couple of Cokes and candy bars.

BEST PICNIC TABLE

Ma Barnes Country Store in Montana. At my lowest point on the ride, Ma Barnes saved the day with cold Cokes, many snack options and an inviting picnic table out front.

Meal Awards

As one might expect, riding more than 100 miles a day through the mountains creates a very hungry motor. I had a lot of good meals along the route. For example, in Basin, Montana, I shared a meal with Alice and Stephan. I enjoyed the food and the company, but it lacked the extra special sauce of a physically hard day or a mentally draining stretch to push it into the "Holy smokes! That was the best food I've had since Grandma's fried chicken and white gravy!" category.

BEST BREAKFAST

Jan's Café in Lima, Montana

BEST LUNCH

El Farolito in El Rito, New Mexico (Hole-in-the-wall with super friendly owners and a great burrito)

BEST DINNER

Boogies in Del Norte, Colorado

Of these, my favorite meal was the breakfast in Lima, Montana. Why was it so special? After all, it was nothing more than a typical "super size me" American breakfast of eggs, pancakes, sausage, and hash browns, with a side of canned peaches. That meal holds a special place in my memory because it was my first real breakfast of the race, and it was the first meal after my first solo camping of the ride. The complete package of great food, friendly staff, and my personal circumstance combined to make it the best breakfast of the entire 2700 miles.

27

Climbing Higher and Higher

L EAVING SARGENTS AND THE TIPI behind, Scotty and I began our eighteenth day in the saddle with a very chilly
road ride. It was over 100 miles to Del Norte, Colorado.

This was the start of the longer resupply stretches that
get longer and longer as the ride travels out of Colorado and
through New Mexico.

Two passes, Cochetopa and Carnero, stood between Sargents
and Del Norte. As was our normal pattern, Scotty and I settled
into different paces as the climbing started. On the way up Cochetopa, I spotted another rider up the road in front of me. I
wondered if I was catching up to a racer who had been ahead of
me?

From a distance, he didn't look like any of the riders that I
had met along the way. As the distance closed between us, I saw
that he was clad in all black. Within a hundred yards of catching
up to him, I could make out his bike and bikepacking bags. I
could tell they did not match any of the Tour Divide riders.
When I caught up to him, he introduced himself as Jerry Hicks.

I recognized the name right away; Jerry was a fellow member of an online endurance group.

Jerry was out on his own multi-day bikepacking trip, finishing up on the Tour Divide route to Del Norte. We chatted about his trip, where he was headed once he arrived in Del Norte, and a bit about my Tour Divide journey. We rode together for the first few miles of the climb.

Feeling a boost, I pulled away from Jerry as the climb switchbacked up and over the top. At the bottom of the ensuing downhill, I stopped for a lunch break under one of the few large trees in the area. A few minutes later, Jerry rode by. It's crazy how you can run into someone on an isolated 100 mile stretch between towns. Had I started the day thirty minutes earlier or later, I may not have run into Jerry at all.

"Hey Jerry, over here," I yelled to him.

"Hey! I didn't think I would see you again."

"Well, I needed to stop to eat and get out of the sun for a bit. Del Norte is still several hours from here."

As we ate, we talked more about his bikepacking trip. This was his final trip before meeting up with his family and then moving overseas for a new job. Our conversation centered on our families, our joys and trying times of being dads, and even how we struggle to balance our bikepacking desires with family time. Talking with Jerry reaffirmed that my decision to stop and see my family in Breckenridge had been the right one.

We headed off down the dirt road looking for a convenient spot to replenish our water supplies. I quickly refilled and started up the final climb before Del Norte. Jerry hung back to filter water using his pump, and I hoped I would run into him again later that night.

Carnero Pass was another Colorado climb - very enjoyable with a gentle grade, open views in the meadows, and aspen trees all around. The downhill was fast and fun. Rolling past the Storm King Campground triggered a memory of Jill Homer's book *Be Brave, Be Strong* where she described coming into the campground well after midnight, exhausted from a really long day. For me, it was early afternoon - way too early to stop for the day. It's interesting how each rider's story varies so much. Thanks to Mother Nature, no two Tour Divide race years are the same, presenting riders with different challenges each year. Every rider has their own unique individual experiences, even those racing together the same year. Jill's welcomed camping spot was simply another road to the left for me.

During this downhill, I noticed the changing landscape. The rock formations were becoming more prevalent and the dirt under my tires was a deeper red.

The final twenty miles into Del Norte were tortuous. While the terrain and route were not all that difficult, I only wanted to get into town and have a meal. I could see Del Norte in the distance. In true Tour Divide fashion, the route took a turn away from the town, leading me up into the hills again. I hit a fun section of doubletrack, and thought, *this isn't so bad.*

... until the doubletrack turned into a deep sand pit - so deep I could only point my bike forward and hope it continued straight. I spun out to the side a few times, but was lucky not to go down. Judging by the state of the sand, other riders must have experienced just as much trouble. Tire tracks went in every direction through the sand. I even found evidence of several big wipeouts still visible.

After the sand pit, the town came into view again. *Almost there. Almost there.* Not exactly. Instead of heading into town, the road took a right turn around the airport. At this point, Del Norte felt more like a mirage than an actual town. Like my dad always says, "You can't get there from here." On one family vacation to Boston, my dad could not figure out how to get us to the USS *Constitution*. We saw the ship many times as my dad drove around downtown Boston, taking every street (except the right one). Similarly, it felt like I would never get to Del Norte.

I rode past the airport and a few more minutes of easy pedaling brought me to the bridge over the Rio Grande River signaling the entrance into Del Norte. Finally! I made it. I stopped at the first gas station I saw to grab a Coke and sit down for a break.

At the gas station, I heard someone yell "Andyyyyyyyy!!!!!" It was Brian Bridau from Ontario, Canada. We first met in Lincoln, Montana, and had crossed paths a few times since then.

"Oh man, it's great to see another rider," Brian exclaimed as he gave me a giant hug.

"Are you doing ok? Good to see you again!" I said.

"I've had a few really rough days. Ended up sleeping right on the side of the road for a couple of nights and I'm just exhausted." Brian replied.

As Brian and I chatted, Jerry Hicks rolled into the gas station, and then a few minutes later, Scotty joined us. The four of us hung out catching up at the gas station before Jerry continued down the road to meet friends for food and beer. We were all jealous of him at that moment.

Brian had already booked a hotel a few blocks away. He invited Scotty and I to split the room with him. It was just after

5:00 p.m. with good weather and hours of daylight left. Should I
decline the hotel, and continue riding? Or stay in town and eat a
big meal and sleep in a bed? If I continued riding, I could make
it part of the way up Indiana Pass - making that climb easier the
following morning. If I stayed, I could enjoy the company of two
fellow riders.

The lure of town and hanging out with Brian and Scotty
won.

As in life itself, there are many little decisions that make up a
2700 mile ride. It's easy to look back and second guess choices
made, such as staying in Del Norte or taking a short day in
Pinedale. Meeting Jerry Hicks along the route is one of the reasons I have no regrets for any of my decisions during the race. If
even one thing had been different, my path would not have
crossed with Jerry's. I would not have eaten breakfast at Brush
Mountain Lodge, or had the mountain lion run in front of me, or
shared a tipi with Scotty. Sure, I may have finished faster. But
that's not everything. I'm content with my race, happy with my
story, and grateful for the encounters I had along the way.

I felt much better about my decision of convenience over
mileage when I sat down for dinner that night at Boogie's Restaurant with Brian and Scotty. Oh, it was a delicious meal -
chicken fried chicken, mashed potatoes, white gravy, vegetable
soup, and a giant piece of pie! And the company made it all the
more enjoyable.

Brian, Scotty, and I shared a grungy hotel room. We discussed our plans for the next day - an early morning ride up Indiana Pass and then on to New Mexico. Before going to sleep, we
started to pack the massive amounts of food we had each purchased at the grocery store. It turned out our eyes were bigger

than our bike bags. Not one of us had enough room on our bikes to pack up all of the goodies we purchased.

We could either eat it or throw it out. Hating to waste food, I indulged in a second dessert of powdered donuts and a candy bar.

Brian, Scotty, and I left Del Norte early the next morning. While there were small outposts along the route, I wouldn't see another town like this for several days, until I'd ridden 190 miles and crossed into New Mexico. Before leaving Del Norte, I was determined to get my fill of coffee. My bike was not leaving town until lots of coffee was consumed.

A few minutes before 5:00 a.m., we rolled up to the same gas station where we met the day before. We waited outside in the cold before the store finally opened twenty minutes late.

Well caffeinated and full of gas station food, the three of us rode out of town, ready to tackle Indiana Pass. The pass takes riders to an elevation of 11,910 feet, the highest point on the Tour Divide. Scotty, Brian, and I gradually split up as the incline started, pedaling at our own pace. Sometimes it's nice to ride with a fellow racer, but it's unwise to keep pace with a faster or slower rider on such a long climb. Instead, I found my own groove and made my way steadily up the pass.

Unlike a lot of climbs in the Rockies, this one hit me hard right from the start, and didn't let up. While I was ready for a long twenty mile grind to the top, the steepness and the chunky gravel road surface caught me off-guard. It takes a lot of energy to stay on your line and not fall over when you are pedaling up a steep climb over chunky gravel at a speed of 4 mph. Each time a tire hit a rock, the bike bounced to one side, requiring me to adjust my steering while I struggled to keep my balance. In the end, I resigned myself to walking the steepest sections of the climb. At this point in the ride, pride took a backseat to forward motion. If I made steady progress throughout the day, I would be in New Mexico by nightfall.

More than four hours after leaving Del Norte, I reached the top of Indiana Pass. I was in the middle of the Rio Grande National Forest at almost 12,000 feet. All around me were mountains, high alpine meadows, small lakes, and another Colorado blue sky. To the west were the towns of Durango and Telluride. Gunnison lay to the north. My route headed south into New Mexico.

After taking a lot of pictures and eating a few snacks, I was prepared for the long downhill into Platoro as I hopped on the bike. Instead, I found a short downhill followed by several more climbs as the route stayed above 11,000 feet. I struggled to pedal up the climbs, reduced to walking once again.

Eventually, the road turned downhill and stretched out before me in the form of a thin ribbon of dirt flanked by multicolored rocky hillsides. My attitude instantly brightened as I began the descent. It turned out there was one other climb to navigate before reaching Platoro. One I had failed to recognize on the map. I found a smooth pedaling groove on my way to the top, and the climb was quite enjoyable.

As the road headed down towards Platoro, several overlooks showed the outpost in the valley below. A welcomed sight made even better by the steep fast downhill that followed. Once I reached Platoro, it was time for a late lunch. The forty-eight-mile ride from Del Norte over Indiana Pass had taken over seven hours to ride.

Platoro is an "outpost," even smaller than Sargents. With no grocery store or gas station, Platoro provides lodging and two restaurants for a lot of four wheelers and hunters. Walking into the Skyline Lodge (the same one where Matthew Lee was filmed eating pancakes by the fire in the *Ride The Divide* movie), I found an open table and immediately ordered another bacon cheeseburger. This bacon cheeseburger came with some tasty green chilies and a gigantic pile of fries. Out of all the burgers I ate, I remember this one as my absolute favorite thanks to the combination of the green chiles and finally being over Indiana Pass on my way to New Mexico.

28

Maps

FROM THE TOP OF A mountain, especially the highest one on the entire ride, logic would tell you that the road should be downhill after the summit. The truth, however, is that while the road must eventually go downhill, it may take a few intermediate climbs before that happens. The key word being eventually. It's a word that is easy to forget when you're tired from hours spent climbing at 4 mph.

Grinding up a hill, even if it takes hours to climb to the top, is something I enjoy. I'm willing to huff and puff, suffering on the uphill to earn the reward of the downhill.

The problem with the Tour Divide is that from time to time I earned the downhill, but the course gave me a teaser instead. I would begin downhill, getting comfortable with the cool wind in my face and taking the corners with speed. Then I would turn one of those corners only to start climbing again. And it wasn't just a little ride that I could coast through or soft pedal over. No, it would be a full-on climb for another half mile or occasionally even several miles. Rookie riders like myself don't know which downhills are in fact teaser downhills.

I used the ACA maps to gauge the upcoming portions of the ride, as well as to plan out my re-supply stops. The maps contain an elevation profile that gives a general idea of the terrain. It's easy to look at a map profile, register the summit and then immediately take your eyes to the bottom of the downhill, envisioning a straight line from top to bottom. In this map viewing tactic, you completely ignore the small yet significant details in between, which may show a flat ridge top, or one of those teaser downhills. For me, I frequently found myself glossing over the map details when the bottom of the downhill ended in a town and my thoughts turned to my next hot meal.

The issue is not that the maps are wrong. Upon closer inspection, the maps do have perfectly clear details that I overlooked. Details that would have been helpful to know when I was perched at the top of the climb, dreaming of a steep and fast downhill. Details that were usually discovered *after* I reached the bottom of the downhill and tried to figure out why the map was "wrong."

You would think that after more than two weeks, I would have figured out my little issue with misinterpreting the maps. There was much more to the maps than simply elevation. The deeper into the route I got, the more I relied on the maps for directions, road intersections, upcoming towns, and re-supply options.

Before the race, I pored over the first three maps, covering Canada, Montana, and part of Wyoming. While analyzing the maps time and time again, I compiled a document of town statistics including restaurant options, lodging options, distance and elevation gain to the next town, and re-supply options in between. The process of studying the maps and compiling my own

version of an atlas helped me memorize most of the details fo
the first 500 miles. In the first week of the race, I rarely consult-
ed the maps.

My map independence was partially due to my pre-race preparation, and also due to the fact that the towns are more fre-
quent in the beginning of the race. Riders typically pass through
multiple towns or outposts each day. Somewhere around Lima,
Montana, the towns begin to get further and further apart, requiring more map reading to know when a supply stop is required. By the time the route reaches New Mexico, not only are
the towns far apart, the options for water become much more
limited, requiring riders to look over the maps in even more detail to ensure adequate water supplies.

All of the pre-race studying and the in-race map consults
reminded me of being a kid on vacation and reading the road
atlas as my dad drove out of South Carolina towards some new
state for vacation. Remember those road atlas books that
showed each state with its roads, interstates, and grids for dis-
tances between cities? It's almost a lost experience now that we
have GPS navigation in our cars and on our phones.

On those long road trips, I remember pulling out the atlas,
opening it to the state we were traveling through, and picking
out roads to see where they would lead. Could I get from Atlanta to St. Louis using only three roads? Could it be done without
interstates? How long does it take to get from St. Louis to Kan-
sas City? It was even more fun when my dad had one of those
large fold out maps with even more detailed roads and land-
marks to incorporate into my "keep yourself busy while on a
road trip" games.

e my frame bag, I had my fold out ACA maps.
the accurate elevation profiles, provided the
.nap did not limit his view to only the top and bot-
. climb and imagine the profile that lay in between.
. .atoro marked the endpoint of the fifth map. Only two maps remained as I approached the drier lands of New Mexico and the promise of pie in Pie Town.

29

Sunsets and Fire

URING LUNCH, MY REVIEW OF the map revealed a slight downhill for twenty miles where the route would take a right turn onto the pavement of Highway 17. Needless to say, after the last forty-eight miles, I was a bit giddy about such a long stretch of "easy riding." It turned out the downhill to Horca was anything but easy or fun. The grade of the road was slightly downhill with a few climbs thrown in for good measure. But the worst part was the road surface - deep, deep gravel and sections of extreme washboard. There was no way to get any speed to coast or even ride in a straight line. There were sections where it would have been tough riding a motorcycle because the gravel was so deep.

About halfway down, the road passed a small campground and snack store. In need of a break from the washboard and frustration of riding through the deep gravel, I stopped. I hoped getting a Coke and resting my hands would help get my mind back to that good place I found in Platoro when I was stuffing my face with fries and a cheeseburger. Didn't happen. The road didn't get any better, and my break didn't really help my mind. I was in of those frustrating, cranky, grumpy moods that my wife would recognize. To make matters worse, after I reached Horca, my GPS died and wouldn't turn back on. Arrggggh!!!

It turns out that my GPS issue was nothing more than dead secondary batteries. I primarily used my dynamo front hub to supply power to the GPS. However, when I wasn't moving fast enough to generate power from the dynamo, the GPS used the secondary batteries. Of course, those batteries had to go dead at the same time I was in a grumpy mood. The Tour Divide keeps on kicking you when you're down.

At the Red Bear restaurant/store, the only store in Horca, I bought batteries, another Coke, and some snacks. The GPS worked again, but I remained grumpy and frustrated. I called my wife and talked to her about the day. Her encouraging words and positive outlook helped reduce my grumpiness like they have done once or twice (ok, maybe more like thousands of times) before.

Leaving Horca, the route follows Highway 17 up La Manga Pass. Being on pavement was a plus, but the climb was steep. Even on pavement, I struggled to find a pedaling rhythm as the full heat of the sunshine in a cloudless sky beat down on me. What a change from the cold and snow I endured just two weeks earlier. I pulled out my headphones for only the third time of the race, and cranked up my "quit whining" playlist.

Before the downhill off of La Manga, the route turns left onto a dirt road that leads into New Mexico. New Mexico! Not only had it been a tough day of riding, but a tough nineteen days to reach the final state of the ride. What's not apparent is that this last state contains more than 700 miles of riding, including some of the toughest roads, climbs, and conditions to be conquered.

A Dream Worth Living

Just past the "entering New Mexico" sign, I sat on a tree stump and soaked in the view of the trees, the blue sky, and silence. The dirt road meandered through the trees slowly climbing up Brazos Ridge.

The sunset as I crested the top of the ridge was a beautiful thing - an array of pinks, blues, and purples lighting up the sky. It's one of those moments that will never escape my mind, just like seeing the sky full of stars atop Fleecer Ridge at midnight, or seeing the thunderstorm building and then enveloping Sarah and me in the Great Basin.

Darkness settled in as I neared the top of the ridge. At this point in the day, my ankles had reached their limit, forcing me to walk in the dark. After the climbing, my mind began to wander, hoping for a downhill. But once again, I had completely misread the map. Brazos Ridge is called a ridge for a good reason - it winds along the top of the mountains for miles, not gaining or losing much elevation, staying above 10,000 feet.

As I walked along the ridge, I was unprotected from the elements, the cold wind a constant presence. I wanted to be off the top of the ridge before I set up camp. I decided a camping spot should be somewhere below 10,000 feet. As soon as the GPS registered 9999 feet, I started scanning the sides of the road for a mostly flat spot with a few trees.

Around 11:00 p.m. and at 9950 feet, a spot came into view. I set up camp and my day ended with 109 difficult miles, short of my 135 mile goal.

The best part of waking up, is a frame bag with Reese's Cups. The original jingle for Folger's sounded and rhymed better, but let me tell you, the taste of an almost frozen Reese's Cup for breakfast is like heaven in a wrapper. Definitely one of the finer tastes along the route.

After eating breakfast and packing up camp, I started up again with a cold ride off of the ridge towards Rio San Antonio where I planned to refill my water. Rio San Antonio is marked on the map with a solid blue line, indicating a flowing river. What I found was a stagnant pool with cows standing in and around it. My water would have to last until Hopewell Lake, twenty miles further down the road.

Water finally arrived after I walked up sections of yet another paved road to Hopewell Lake. I was getting really good at walking my mountain bike on pavement. The day was turning out to be quite hot, the first time in the entire ride where heat became an issue. After a quick stop to refill my water and eat lunch, I got back in the saddle and pushed on.

I don't remember a lot about the section from Hopewell Lake to Cañon Plaza. The weather was hot and my legs were dead. I seriously debated ending my race in Pie Town. While Pie Town was only a few hundred miles from the finish, it seemed I would never get to that Mexico border. With only a handful of days left, every little setback felt magnified. Not only was I ready to be back home with my family, but I was behind my target finish, and my dad would have to wait in a hotel for several days before picking me up.

My saving grace for the day turned out to be the roadside stand in Cañon Plaza, featured in *Ride The Divide*. After seeing the movie, it felt like déjà vu - it looks the same, and Sylvia is just as nice in person. We sat and chatted as I ate candy bars - the ride, her kids, a bug outside the building, the trash man as he drove by, the weather. Very ordinary conversation, but ex-

actly what I needed at that moment. Thanks to Sylvia's grati-
tude and smiles, the pedal strokes became much easier.

The long climb out of Cañon Plaza towards El Rito features a
lot of pine trees and sand that took me back to my early cycling
days in South Carolina, particularly the trails at Sesquicenten-
nial State Park. But the feeling of the Southeast was short lived.
Once I crested the climb, the terrain shifted to the desert-like
small bushes that provided no shade.

In El Rito, I stopped at a tiny Mexican restaurant for a late
lunch. Oh boy, was it delicious! No bacon cheeseburgers in sight!
Instead, a giant burrito, sopapillas, and coffee; a nice change in
pace. As I ate, the owner stopped by my table.

"How is everything?" he asked.

"Excellent! Everything is great," I replied.

"Are you riding over Polvadera into Cuba?"

"Yes."

"There is a fire burning up there. It might be in the area you
are riding," he said.

"That's not good," I said.

"Check with the Forest Service office across the street. They
can tell you if there are any road closures," he said.

"Thank you for letting me know about the fire," I said.

"Good luck and be safe."

I ate the sopapillas after drenching them with honey, and
then rode across the street to the Ranger station. They confirmed that there were road closures on the Tour Divide route.

I planned to camp up on the ridge between Abiquiu and Cuba, but with a fire burning, my new plan was to reassess the situation at Abiquiu. The road to Abiquiu is paved and slightly
downhill. Even with the headwind I faced, I pedaled at a fast

pace. I can only imagine how fun that section could be with a nice tailwind.

In Abiquiu, I stopped at the gas station for food, water, and fire updates. A sign on the door mentioned the road closures - the exact road the route followed. I texted Matthew Lee, the race coordinator, about the closures. According to Matthew, other people were currently up there riding, and he wasn't aware of any closures.

I may be crazy, but I was not eager to ride into an active fire area. Living in Colorado, I've seen how fires can take off with no warning, consuming thousands and thousands of acres in a matter of hours. The wind was gusting and I didn't feel comfortable going up on the Polvadera Mesa outside of Abiquiu.

While I was sitting outside the gas station contemplating my next move, my friend Nic rolled up. We had not seen each other since the second day of the race, and it was great to meet up with him again. Neither of us wanted to ride into the fire area; instead we checked into the Abiquiu Inn to rest and figure out a plan for the next day. My riding day ended at 5:00 p.m. with only eighty-three miles covered, putting me even further behind my planned finish date.

It felt like my final finish time was getting pushed out by the hour. But stopping in Abiquiu gave Nic and I the opportunity to catch up on all we had been through in the last three weeks. We were on the same ride, but each had unique experiences to share. Now we had a chance to ride together for the last 560 miles to the finish, pushing our limits past what we thought was possible.

30

Resistance

S TEVEN PRESSFIELD, IN HIS BOOK *The War of Art*, describes the "Resistance" (yes it gets a capital letter) as:

"Resistance cannot be seen, touched, heard, or smelled. But it can be felt. We experience it as an energy field radiating from a work-in-potential. It's a repelling force. It's negative. Its aim is to shove us away, distract us, prevent us from doing our work."

The beast that is Resistance waits to pounce on us once we get to work or strive for goals. The only way through it is to fight it and push it away from our minds. Easier said than done, of course.

Where was Resistance in my Tour Divide experience?

It was the fear surrounding the first day with the potential for bears and riding alone into the unknown.

The voice inside telling me to stay in Seeley Lake after riding only thirty miles for the day.

The apprehension of camping solo for the first time.

The desire to stop racing once I reached Pie Town, so close to my final goal.

These feelings are the complete opposite of my son's "I Got This" mantra. Pushing past the doubts is the only way make it over to the "I Got This" side of pursuit.

But Resistance finds a way to escape from its cage to become an even greater beast the closer we are to our goal. The attacks carry more force.

That's where I found myself as I rode through New Mexico. Entering the final state after almost three weeks of struggling for forward progress should have been a happy moment. Instead, I let my guard down thinking that I was nearing the finish, even though there were hundreds of miles left to travel. Resistance broke out of its cage, transforming itself into a monkey on my back, a strong wind trying to push me back into Colorado, and let's not forget the serpent silently putting negative thoughts into my mind.

Fighting off the monkey on my back was the easy part. It was slightly more difficult to cut through the wind to make progress. But that damned serpent talking in my head proved to be the most evil form of the Resistance. It kept telling me to think about cruising to the finish and how I was almost done, trying to let my guard down.

It got so bad, that I even had thoughts of finishing the race in Pie Town as I sat on a porch eating slices of pie and scoops of ice cream. I figured my dad, who likes pie and ice cream as much as me, would enjoy the porch time. I'd already ridden over 2400 miles so why did I need to finish?

"Stop it!" I would say to the serpent.

"Mmmm, pie would be good."

"That's crazy!" I yelled back.

"Imagine eating ice cream and pie while resting with your feet up."

"No, I will finish this race!" came my final response as I pushed down a little harder on the pedals.

The Resistance was having a field day within my mind. Of course I wasn't going to stop that close to the finish. Back in Montana I had resolved myself to finish even if it involved injuries to myself. Now, I was thinking of stopping short because I wanted to have pie while sitting on a porch?

Sorry Resistance, but that's not going to work.

As Mr. Pressfield once again described you –

"Most of us have two lives. The life we live, and the unlived life within us. Between the two stands Resistance."

I pushed Resistance aside, down the cliff and into the deep dark bushes to live out my dream of finishing the Tour Divide.

Of course my win would be short lived. Resistance would climb back up the hillside and intercept me on my way to Pie Town. He's like an old Timex watch that takes a licking and keeps on ticking. He's like Rocky Balboa who can seemingly be out for the count before getting up and coming back for a last minute knockout.

Somewhere in the heat, rain, and miles of mud in the coming days, Resistance would surprise me. Add in equal parts of late nights, sore swollen ankles, and the ever present prospect of running out of food and water, and you have a breeding ground for an even stronger response by Resistance. But try as Resistance might, I was not going to back down.

31

Gilligan's Island

W E AWOKE READY FOR A relatively easy ride from Abiquiu to Cuba. The day begin with a big breakfast at the hotel, and we planned a short eighty mile day before the final push to the finish. My expectations were a little off. It wasn't a short ride, and it certainly wasn't an easy cruise.

The day started off calm enough, with a later than normal wake-up and a casual breakfast at the hotel restaurant. The Abiquiu Inn was a nice place to stay, eat, and recharge. Almost too nice. It was easy for Nic and I to lounge over breakfast while I downed cup after cup of coffee. The coffee was my rocket fuel for the long climb up the Polvadera Mesa, labelled the toughest climb of the route by many a Tour Divide racer. (Of course, I had somehow overlooked that fact with my expectation of an easy cruise over the Mesa and into Cuba. Why, oh why, do I do these things?)

After leaving the Inn on Highway 84, the route turns left onto a smaller paved road. The road steadily climbs to the edge of town where it becomes steeper, eventually turning to dirt. My climbing legs returned, ready to power me up and over one of the longest climbs on the Tour Divide. The only issue turned out to be the humidity. I expected typical New Mexico air; as dry as a field that hasn't seen rain in several months. On this day, it was extremely humid, to the point where I was sweating buckets within the first couple of miles of the climb. It felt like I had been transported back to South Carolina, riding on an August afternoon along the muddy river sections at Harbison State Forest. At least there weren't SC mosquitos to deal with.

Just like that, my climbing legs left me. The combination of the heat and humidity had me pedaling slower minute by minute. I was probably only halfway up this long climb when I really started to feel bad. In my infinite wisdom when planning for an easy day, I only filled my water to half capacity, to save weight on my bike. I realized I had gone through at least two-thirds of my water in only a few miles. I don't think I've ever gone through so much water in such a short distance. It was the first time (and definitely the last) that I failed to fill my water carrying capacity. Assuming it was an easy day ahead was a big mistake. You know what they say about making assumptions. This was just one of several issues I would face on the Polvadera Mesa.

The heat, humidity, and rationing of water had me feeling really bad as we neared the top of the climb. I needed a break. We found a shady spot that even had a couple of downed trees for a makeshift bench. After resting and eating lunch, I felt better. My GPS indicated several streams in the next few miles. Surely I could remedy my water shortage at one of them.

Not on this day.

The top of the climb was only a mile or two ahead. Unfortunately for me, this was one of those Tour Divide climbs that didn't follow with a steep downhill where you could recover from the long climb. Instead, I continued to pedal along the top of the mesa with rolling hills for the next ten miles. It's a horrible kind of torture when you've lost your energy and are running out of water. I didn't think it could get much worse...

...until it began to rain and hail. This was turning into *Gilligan's Island* before my eyes. The weather was getting rough, but unlike Gilligan, we were not getting lost. We could see exactly where we needed to go - right into more clouds and rain.

Way back on the second day in the Canadian Flathead Valley, it was easy to stay motivated as we all rode through the freezing cold, wet conditions. Even with frozen wet feet, it was early in the race. It was even comical once my feet were so cold and soaked. One more drenching wasn't going to hurt. I could either embrace the "suck" factor or be completely miserable. My excitement to reach the border certainly helped me embrace the brutality.

Now we were almost three weeks into the race, and embracing the suck factor was not as easy. Up on the mesa, as the hail pelted my exposed arms and legs, I could only yelp and curse each time a big hail stone stung me. It hurt. It sucked. Still, Nic and I managed to laugh at our situation as it sunk in that we were becoming Gilligan with each passing wave of rain and hail.

The third wave of hail hit us while we rode a downhill section, with the sting of the hail hitting our skin becoming too much to continue on. We ducked under the cover of a large pine tree to wait for the hail to subside.

"Hey Nic, how's your cruise going up to Cuba?" I asked in between chuckles.

"Oh, it's just an easy, simple eighty-mile day. It's awesome." he said.

"It's a pleasure cruise, right?" I asked through even more laughs.

"Yeah, you know, just a little bit of overheating and sweating, then a little bit of pelting by hail."

"And running out of water by lunch. Just a beautiful day."

When the hail let up, we hopped back on our muddy, soaking steeds, pedaling on towards the fire area. A single police car sat at the intersection of two Forest Service roads. While the official route was still technically open, Matthew Lee had outlined an alternate route option. This alternate took the road to the left, looped to the south, and bypassed the fire area. We opted for the alternate.

We were surrounded by rain and water. I carried an empty hydration bladder, having run out of drinking water long ago. The irony of the moment was not lost on me - I could see water everywhere, but I couldn't drink any of it. With another twenty miles yet to ride before reaching Cuba, I stopped to fill up my hydration bladder at the side of the road. I found a brown muddy mess of water where a stream normally flowed. The rain caused dirt to run off and mix with the stream water. I filled up a liter of water, which probably contained half dirt and half water. Luckily, I used a Sawyer filter so the dirty water wasn't an issue.

The first sip of my water had a definite dirt taste to it. But it was water which I needed.

Initially, the bypass route was an easier ride with some downhills and little in the way of climbing. Once it met up with the paved State Highway 126 that led to Cuba, all of those downhill sections came back to haunt me as I climbed back up to rejoin the official Tour Divide route.

It was good to finally get through the fire area. Because of my cautious approach to fires, I lost at least a half day. This race was starting to drag on too long. I was in that weird place where you are so close to your goal while at the same time it feels like the goal is slowly pulling away from you. While I didn't feel comfortable sleeping near an active fire area and I stopped for the night in Abiquiu, other riders rode through the area without incident. I'm sure other years have seen racers placed in much more severe fire situations. We each make our own decisions on this ride. In the end, I'm content with my choice to stop, even though I would love to have that half day back.

My struggles of the day were rewarded with an incredibly fast and fun paved downhill into Cuba. With the wide sweeping turns, I could tuck down into the aero bars and just let gravity push me faster and faster, right up to the limit of my abilities. There is a fine line between exhilaration and crashing. I certainly didn't want to crash on a paved downhill and have my Tour Divide dream end so close to the finish. But simply cruising into town and not enjoying the fun downhill was not in my DNA. So, yeah, I tucked into the aero bars and let it fly as my speed increased, surging past 45 mph on the steepest sections. As an added bonus, I outran the approaching storm and made it to a Mexican restaurant, ready for my next meal.

At the restaurant, Andy Lawrence was finishing up his dinner before he headed out on the paved section towards Grants. It must have been around 6:00 p.m.; the sun was just starting to duck behind the mountains.

Stay in a cheap hotel or continue to ride? While I wanted to continue to push for the finish, there were reasons to stop for the night. A looming storm was sure to bring rain. From my Tour Divide route research, I knew the upcoming section lacked places to camp on the side on the road, and this stretch was not always cyclist-friendly. We decided to err on the side of caution and get a hotel room. After all, what was one more night?

While sitting in the restaurant for dinner, my ankles swelled up even more, and it became painful to walk. After a slow trudge to reach the grocery store a few blocks away, I indulged myself in all kinds of junk food and coffee drinks for the next day's ride.

32

Mind Games

ON WHAT I ASSUMED WOULD be an easy day, everything became the complete opposite. It felt like an episode of *Gilligan's Island* where the *S.S. Minnow* was lost, complete with a comedy of errors between Gilligan and the Captain. The stretch between Abiquiu and Cuba ended up being one of the harder days on the route. Getting through days like that (and, at times, even just a half mile section) were often an exercise in mind over matter. Actually, it was more along the lines of playing mind games to keep myself from focusing on the hard tasks that were staring me in the face.

While riding 2700 miles, I managed to build my own gaming system between my GPS and my head. It was necessary to keep me moving forward without the use of my iPod. One goal I had coming into the ride was not to zone out too much with my iPod. I wanted to enjoy the scenery, live in the moment, and not rely on the music to get through the day. Mission accomplished. My music only came out four times during the race (Red Meadow Pass, leaving Rawlins, WY, climbing up La Manga Pass, and the final miles to Antelope Wells).

I guess I could have sung out loud, but I have this weird problem of not remembering more than a couple of lines to a song. That will drive anyone crazy if they have to hear themselves repeating a few words over and over for sixteen hours a day. I had a bout of this back in Montana when I couldn't get the chorus of "You Make Beautiful Things" by Gungor out of my head. During one of my phone calls home early in the race, one of my kids told about singing that song at Vacation Bible School. Of course, he sung it a few times for me, which caused it to stick in my brain. Once was enough. I couldn't go for thousands of miles repeating the partial lyrics from a handful of songs I could remember without hearing the music.

To combat the craziness that could crop up in my head, I made up my own GPS games. During a tough stretch, whether that was a long demanding climb or just a bad spot mentally, I played with the zoom level on the GPS map display. The game started with a zoom level that held my goal just outside the edge of the screen. Forward progress brought my goal into view on the edge of the screen. That triggered the next zoom level, making the goal once again vanish off the screen. This process repeated itself until my goal was finally reached.

On some long climbs, it would be hours of pedaling, making slow progress before the summit icon and my actual position became one. At times it was maddening because the icon would not come back on screen nearly fast enough. What really turns you batty is when you end up walking up a climb and having the zoom levels feel like they were never going to change. Walking up a climb at night in the dark was even worse. Now that I write this, maybe playing the mind games wasn't the smartest idea after all.

For the most part, the games kept my mind busy enough to not focus on how long the climb was or how tired I was from pedaling and pedaling and pedaling. The twenty-mile climbs felt shorter with the games being played.

Food also became a player in my mind games. It wasn't anything along the lines of seeing if I could eat the Old 96er or two full plates of food in one sitting. My snacks became rewards as I rode. During the race, I never ran out of food or even had to ration my food. I'm sure I would not be talking about mind games centered around food had I actually run out during the race.

My go-to food for eating while riding was Orange Slices. Oh no, it wasn't the real thing. It was the sugar coated gummy-type slices. A bag a day keeps healthy food away. My bag o' slices was always within easy reach at the top of my gas tank bag. On some of the long stretches of pavement and even on some of the long climbs, I wouldn't let myself have free access to the orange slices. Instead, each yummy slice had to be earned (think about the old EF Hutton commercials) by reaching a mile marker, seeing the summit icon on my GPS, or reaching some visual landmark.

It was part keeping the mind busy and part keeping constant calories coming into my body. For some reason, I never got into super deep thought during the ride. I had a few moments, but nothing sustained over a day or several days. I was a bit surprised by this because I had fully expected the long days to find me lost in deep thought.

My orange slices and GPS games gave me enough to keep my mind occupied.

Getting to see the summit icon on the GPS or eating that final orange slice for the climb meant one thing. I could look forward to the long downhills causing me to drop like a rock into places like Cuba, New Mexico.

33

What About the Pie?

SINCE SO MANY NIGHTS WERE spent in hotels during the first week of the race, I really wanted Abiquiu to be the last hotel until the finish. But you know what they say about the best laid plans. We would have one last hotel stay in Cuba.

In the hotel, Nic and I came up with an ambitious plan to finish the Tour Divide in three monster days. Of course, our plan involved riding 165 miles per day, something neither of us had ever done for multiple days in a row. And especially not after taking a beating for three weeks on the Tour Divide. But hey, you have to dream big, right?

It turned out Scotty and Brian were also at the hotel. Our riding styles and routines were quite different, and I didn't see them during the day very often, but we continued to finish in the same location each night. Scotty and Brian had changed their days to get up and start riding before sunrise to beat the afternoon heat. My approach was still the same - try to get up with the sunrise and make sure to get a full night's sleep. Regardless of our approach, we were covering the same ground each day.

Inside the hotel, I could see the swelling in my lower leg was worse. As soon as I took my sock off, the swelling migrated down to cover my calf and entire ankle. Nic urged me to start a treatment of heat and ice. After several rounds of "treatment" using the trashcan as an improvised bucket, my legs felt better. Not well enough for 150+ mile days, but better. I knew there was a limit to how far I could push them each day. What was that limit? 50, 100, or 150 miles?

Because the hotel did not have a coffee maker, I purchased a couple of canned coffee drinks the night before. Caffeine was a major requirement for the next few "monster mileage" days. I tucked a few 5 Hour Energy drinks into my frame bag for any caffeine "emergencies." I had learned my lesson when crossing into Colorado on several days of no caffeine, and wouldn't make that mistake again.

The alarm began ringing at 5:30 a.m. One microwaved burrito and two cold coffee drinks later, I was ready for the longest section of pavement on the route - 120 miles to Grants, New Mexico. I had no complaints about a long day of pavement. I hoped it would give my ankle a bit of a break.

The initial miles out of Cuba have some rolling hills that are perfect for tucking into the aero bars and finding a rhythm. Sure, it's a steady cadence but where's the fun in that? Nic always has a smile and finds ways to make the riding fun. Instead of ticking away mile after mile, we managed to fit in a few sprints to the top of the hills, enjoying our time on the bike. It was the only time on the ride where I goofed around. Sprinting and pushing hard may not have been the smartest idea, but sometimes fun is better than smart.

On the map, there are three stores listed on the road to Grants. We stopped at the first one, forty miles into the day, to top off our water and buy a few more snacks. It was July 4th just before 8:00 a.m. in the morning. The outside of the store didn't make a great first impression, especially with the bars on the windows. However, once inside the store, it was clean and well lit, with wide aisles and a huge selection of snacks. After having lived out of gas stations for the previous three weeks, I was becoming a good judge of gas station quality. This store was the nicest one along the entire route.

Everyone that came into the store said hello to us; one woman even said hello from across the store. New Mexico certainly had the roughest, rundown towns along the route. But the old saying "don't judge a book by its cover" was certainly true. Both the gleaming interior of the store and the friendly people reminded me of this adage on that Fourth of July morning.

We knew this would be the hottest day of the ride so far. We rode past Pueblo Pintado where everything was closed and our hopes for a lunch stop were dashed. It turned out that stopping at the first store was a very wise choice. The rest of the day was desolate with no services, as the other two stores listed on the ACA maps had closed down. The first store was our only opportunity for water or food until reaching the outskirts of Grants more than eighty miles away.

I thought "heat" would be the word of the day, until a group of dogs changed that word to "chase." Nic was in front of me by about fifty yards as we rode past a house on the left. From the house, we heard barking and then five large dogs appeared. Being in front, Nic was well past the house before the dogs bolted

under the fence without slowing down and ran down the embankment onto the road. As second man, I was right in their
path. The first four dogs that ran onto the road didn't worry me.
When I saw the face and snarl on the fifth dog as he darted under the fence, I got worried. He was only interested in one thing
and it wasn't a nice tummy rub. My ankles and legs were going
to be tasty as he bit me.

I ratcheted up my cadence, spinning my legs to generate
more speed. The dogs gave chase, but I managed to surge away
from them and avoid an altercation. Nic was so worried about
me, he pulled out his camera at his safe distance to take pictures
of my escape from the jaws of the viscous fifth dog. When I
caught up to him, he was laughing quite loudly.

"Dude, that was close. That fifth dog was really going for
me," I said.

"At least I got it on camera. I didn't have a chance to zoom in
before I took it so I hope it turns out ok."

I responded with, "I think I'll ride in the front now so the
next set of dogs can go after you!"

An hour later, we contemplated a lunch break and looked for
a place to get out of the sunshine. That is, until we noticed more
dogs off to the right-hand side. This time it was a pack of dogs,
just like you would see a pack of wolves or coyotes.

"Let's keep riding and hope they don't notice us." Nic said.

"Yeah, they don't look like they belong to anyone. It's a pack
of wild dogs," I said quietly.

After being chased by "domestic" dogs, I had no interest in
facing a wild pack.

The dogs were a few hundred yards away, walking around an
abandoned shack of a house. It was obvious no one lived in the

house, or anywhere close by. The dogs looked mean, dirty, and did I mention mean? Each time one of them moved their head, we hoped it didn't look up in our direction and notice us. Their chase would have been much harder to outrun.

We managed to get past the dogs without incident, and continued to ride for a few miles before stopping to eat our lunch of gas station food without any shade cover.

Options for getting out of the heat are limited when it's high noon with nothing but rolling hills and scrubby bushes all around. No cliffs to provide a bit of shade, and certainly no large trees to sit under. Opportunity for shade finally came when the road went through a short tunnel at the Peabody Energy mine. When shade trees don't exist, tunnels are the next best thing! We sat down in the wide shoulder of the road, resting against the wall of the tunnel as we enjoyed a short break from the sunshine.

All good things must come to an end. We still had forty miles to Grants, all in the heat of the day. I tried to find a comfortable pace on the climbs, coast on the downhills, and take in the mile upon mile of desolate terrain laid out before me.

Eventually, the road became a long gentle downhill as it approached the intersection to Highway 605. Up ahead, a thunderstorm was building over the San Mateo Mountains.

The wind picked up with the clouds getting closer and darker by the minute. We thought for sure we were going to get soaked just a few short miles from Grants. With rain gear deployed, we were as ready as we could be. Somehow, the storm stayed up on the ridge, and we stayed dry as we rode into town on Route 66. We stopped at a Dairy Queen for some well-earned ice cream.

In the 1960's driving along Route 66 was quite the experience. Many families in station wagons loaded down with luggage drove the route to experience the western states. Downtowns were full of stores, restaurants, and hotels for the travelers.

Unfortunately, the grandeur of Route 66 has been lost in Grants. Now, it's a bunch of ramshackle buildings, remnants of their former selves, hinting at the one-time glory that was once Route 66.

Towards the east end of town, we spotted Blake's Lotaburger, an old-school burger joint that reminded me of a place my dad used to take my brother and me when we worked with him as kids. At Blake's, a counter lined the windows where Nic and I sat down to eat. We watched the cars and people go by on their way to Fourth of July parties, but there would be no celebrations for us.

Instead, we focused on our re-supply for the 260 mile stretch between Grants and Silver City, the longest stretch of the entire route. Pie Town was only seventy miles away. However, based on our expected ride times, we weren't sure if we would arrive when the cafés were open. A real pity if you ask me. A pie, any pie, would have been welcomed after riding more than 2000 miles.

Inside the first gas station we found, we proceeded to load up on anything and everything that resembled food. The cashier rang me up, and my haul tallied $72. Yes, I spent $72 on gas station food. I was determined not to run out of food. My purchase had to last me for two days before I expected to arrive in Silver City.

"Are you sure we should do this?" I pondered. "It's a lot of food and I don't even know if it will all fit..."

Every nook and cranny on my frame bag, seat bag, and handlebar bag was stuffed with some type of food. A Coke and a Gatorade barely made it into my seat bag. The frame bag had muffins and candy bars smooshed into the last available space. My portable backpack was packed to its limit and there were a few items that did not fit.

"We could hang out in Pie Town to wait for stores to open. Although, I really want to keep going," was Nic's reply.

"I know. But, man, we're going to miss out on the pie!"

"We should keep riding and see how it turns out. Nothing we can do about it right now," he said.

Nic was right. Pie or no pie, we had to get to Pie Town first. After eating the last items that wouldn't fit into my bag and talking to my wife on the phone for a few minutes, Nic and I headed out of town on our overloaded bikes. At least the bikes and packs would get lighter as we ate and drank our way to Silver City.

We had already covered 120 miles for the day; our goal was to ride another fifty miles before camping for the night. Most of those miles were paved as the route travelled south through the El Malpais National Monument.

The sandstone bluffs on our left became washed in pinks and purples as the sky turned from light blue to cobalt and finally into a deep navy. The moon slowly rose up over the bluffs, spreading it's light through the thin layer of clouds.

Once the pavement ended and we took the turn towards Pie Town, the road turned into an extremely washboarded and sandy mess. A couple of times, I had to walk through the sand because I got bogged down or thrown off track. It was a frustrating pattern of smooth dirt for a few feet, then some really rough washboard, and then a stretch of deep sand to round it out.

"How are you able to ride through this mess?" I asked Nic.

It was a question asked in frustration, but one where I already knew the answer. He was simply an amazing technical rider that floated over obstacles. Before the race, we had ridden on part of the Colorado Trail with a few other guys. There were very steep sections scattered with rock after rock. All of us tried and failed to get more than halfway up the rocky sections. Nic rode up those pitches on a fully loaded bike with the calmest and steadiest pedal stroke I have ever seen. While the rest of us were bouncing off of our intended lines and hanging on for every foot of forward progress, Nic cruised up hitting every line as if it was flat pavement. No wonder he seemed to glide through the sand pits and washboard on the dirt road.

After a few miles of the sand traps and washboards, even Nic began to get frustrated. It had been a long day. In the dark, battered by the road, nothing was fun at that point.

"The camping spots should be close by. I can't take much more of this. I need to stop," I said.

"That's probably a good idea," Nic's responded. "What about here? This should work."

"Yeah," I agreed. "We just need a flat spot off the road. No need to go any further."

"Ok," Nic's voice tailed off as he was already walking his bike into an open area with no bushes or trees. It was the perfect camping spot for two weary riders.

Within a few minutes, Nic had his tent setup and I had my tarp pitched. We were definitely in desert-like territory now. The sand was very fine, and I was concerned about my skinny titanium tent stakes. Would they have enough holding power in such soft conditions? But this was our spot for the night, and it would have to do. Worst case, I'd be doing some cowboy camping under the stars if the stakes came out and the tarp fell down.

A final late night snack and I was soon asleep. At 163 miles, I had ridden the longest mileage day of my life. If I wanted to finish the race in two more days, it meant that each day would have to be a similar distance. Could I manage my three longest riding days after three weeks of racing and an ankle that was swelling more with each passing day?

The morning sunrise accompanied by a soft pattering of rain created a nice rainbow to greet the day. Breakfast was a smooshed gas station pastry and a Coke. You know, standard nutritious fare that fuels a body for 150 miles of riding.

Gentle rain continued to fall as we broke down our campsite and headed on towards Pie Town. While there were a few remaining sand traps to navigate, the road became steadily better as we rode.

Enjoying the smoother road, Nic called out, "Hey, is that an elk over there to the left?"

"There aren't elk around here, are there? Seems like we are too far south." I replied.

"Yeah, but there was that sign back there that mentioned an elk crossing."

"Oh wow, you're right. That is an elk," I confirmed as the elk raised his head and we saw the antlers. We realized there were, in fact, three elk.

Three elk, a rainbow, and the end of the sand trap - the day was off to a good start. Turning backwards we saw Scotty and

Brian riding up the road and we waited for them to catch up to us.

"Hey guys, fancy seeing you here," I said as they rode up to us.

"Hey, how are you?" Scotty asked.

"We're good, great morning so far. You doing ok?"

"Except for that nasty sand and washboard back there. That was hard to ride in the dark last night," Scotty said.

"Same here. We got through the worst of it and called it a night. We must have camped very close to each other," I said.

Scotty and Brian pulled out food for a second breakfast. Nic and I said our goodbyes and continued riding. In front of us were the rolling hills that would take us to Pie Town. It would be a sad day; we were due to arrive in town in the morning, and the cafés didn't open until the afternoon. After riding over 2000 miles, there was going to be no pie in Pie Town. We reached the highway crossing in Pie Town and stopped to consider our options.

"Can we really ride through Pie Town without eating pie?" I asked.

"We still have a lot of food from Grants," Nic said. "I don't know if we need to stop."

"I know, but..."

"We can either ride through or wait a few hours for a shop to open. But I don't really want to waste time," Nic said. "I'd rather keep going. I want to finish tomorrow."

"I want to finish tomorrow, too. But I also want pie," I replied with a smile.

As we talked, a car pulled up and a silver haired woman in a brightly colored sundress stepped out.

"Hey there! What are your names?" she asked.

We introduced ourselves, and in return we were greeted with a warm hug. Nita owned the Toaster House in Pie Town. Formerly her house, she had converted it into a hostel for cyclists on the Great Divide Mountain Bike Route and hikers on the Continental Divide Trail (CDT).

"Follow me. There's food at the house!" she said.

That morning I feasted on coffee, applesauce, and frozen pizza. An exquisite meal even though it was a strange combination of foods. And the best part? There was pie in Pie Town after all! Nita brought out a banana coconut pie and cut us each a generous size slice.

As I stuffed my face with pie, Nita told stories of previous cyclists and hikers. I was so engrossed in the moment, I almost didn't see Scotty and Brian roll up to join our pie party. They were just as happy to see the Toaster House as we had been. They started with pie and then finished with a frozen pizza of their own. We were all smiling and thankful for Nita's hospitality before tackling the Gila Wilderness.

34

Trail Angels

FROM THE MOMENT SHE GREETED Nic and I with a gigantic hug down to the last wave goodbye as we left, Nita had a smile on her face. It's similar to the hospitality shown by Kirsten at Brush Mountain Lodge. With Kirsten, it was a friendly cookout style hospitality. With Nita, it was a motherly nurturing hospitality. One where you could tell she wanted you to come in, stay a while, enjoy a meal, and leave feeling better than when you arrived.

Walking into the house, I could feel the footprints of the hikers and cyclists that have been through the house throughout the years. Over our meal, we talked about our own race and Nita told stories of raising her family in the house, the tragedy of losing a child, and how she turned the house into a hostel after her kids were grown.

When our conversation somehow turned to cell phones, TV news, and technology, Nita's response was perfect. "That's why I live in Pie Town. To get away from all of that!" she quipped with a smile.

She could open her windows and look out to see the mountains, trees, and breathe the fresh air instead of getting bogged down with other topics. Can't really argue with that idea.

On the outside wall, there are many shoes hanging up from past hikers. Some look new and others had been worn bare with holes throughout. Sitting on the deck looking at the shoes got me thinking about the miles all of the people have hiked and biked along these trails, and of their experiences. Many of the sweetest and comforting miles were because of places like the Toaster House.

Before leaving, we received another round of strong hugs from Nita. We left with full stomachs, raised spirits, and a love for the great people along the route. An hour earlier, Nita was a complete stranger who stopped her car to talk with two dirty, smelly cyclists, dejected at the prospect of riding 2000+ miles only to miss out on pie in Pie Town. Now, we had a bond and my heart would be forever touched by a woman who opened her house to anyone, no questions asked.

Nita at the Toaster House and Kirsten at Brush Mountain Lodge were two of the many trail angels I encountered during the race. It wasn't outside support or special treatment that made them trail angels. Instead, it was their outpouring of hospitality and willingness to smile while giving a hug to a racer.

Throughout the race, each and every day brought someone that took a few minutes to chat, or a nod as I rode my bike alongside their F-250, or small talk before ordering a meal at a restaurant. On days where I rode solo, the connections felt a bit stronger. There is definitely a pull to have a connection with people and have a conversation, even if your own solitude time doesn't bother you.

In addition to Nita and Kirsten, I encountered other trail angels during my race.

Rocky in Elkford, British Columbia who opened his gym to us the first night rather than having us stay at the hotel.

The hotel clerk in Eureka, Montana who allowed a bunch of wet and tired racers to crash on the floor of the lounge for a few hours.

The staff at Holland Lake Lodge provided to-go PB&J sandwiches in place of the high-end breakfast and lunch that I couldn't stay to enjoy.

The town of Ovando, Montana, welcomed every racer as they crested the hill into town.

The anonymous owner of the snack table who left bags of Swedish Fish, dried mangoes, and trail mix outside of Helena, Montana.

The grandfather at Squirrel Creek Lodge outside of Yellowstone who opened his doors a few minutes early to prepare me a hearty breakfast.

Sylvia and her shady, well stocked Snack Shack in Cañon Plaza, New Mexico.

These are just a few of the many encounters. After a long day of riding or a wet night of camping, it's uplifting to meet people with a friendly smile and caring attitude, even if only for a few seconds. Most of them probably didn't even know how much they helped this weary rider with their simple actions.

35

Wrestling the Gila Monster

L EAVING A TOWN AFTER SITTING down to a big meal always makes the riding more enjoyable. The miles of
climbing while heading back into the mountains ticked off
with relative ease while I looked around at the scenery,
listened to the sounds of the forest, and pedaled with refreshed
legs. After crossing Highway 12, about thirty-five miles south of
Pie Town, the easy riding ended. The roads deteriorated into a
washboard torture.

To make matters worse, a storm was building. Based on our
direction, we were headed towards some wet riding in the Gila
National Forest, exactly the place I didn't want to encounter
rain and mud.

Between the clouds and the rough road, things were not
looking good. It was then that Nic introduced me to his cattle
guard game. For you city folks, a cattle guard is a metal grate
spanning the road to prevent cattle from crossing. Along the
Tour Divide, there are hundreds of cattle guards that are
crossed. Nic, being the fun spirited person, devised a game out
of the crossings. Instead of simply rolling over them as most riders do, the game was to see if the bike could line up with one of

the 3" metal strips that ran in the same direction as the road. If you could line up both tires to roll over the strip without hitting the perpendicular pipes, you score a point. Nic scored on almost every crossing, even at night and in the rain. Me? I was decent and scored on about seventy percent of the cattle guards. With so many cattle guards, the game broke up the long tiring miles as we got closer to the Gila.

At the last house before entering the Gila, we heard gunshots in the distance. Never a good sound when you are traveling along an empty dirt road on a bicycle. As I got closer to the house, I heard a man yell towards us "Hey, you guys got enough water?"

"Yes, we have plenty," I replied.

"Are you sure? It's a dry stretch," he yelled back.

"We have plenty to get us to Beaverhead. Thank you."

"Ok, be safe and enjoy your ride."

"Thanks. Enjoy your afternoon," I said.

As we passed the house and came upon the sign indicating the entrance to the Gila Wilderness, it felt like we were riding into a monster's lair. Just inside the lair, we stopped to sit on a log to eat lunch before climbing deeper into the grips of the Gila.

The Gila National Forest covers 3.3 million acres. Within the boundaries of the forest are three designated wilderness areas. The largest of these is the Gila Wilderness, covering over 550,000 acres while also holding the distinction of becoming the world's first wilderness area in 1924. Within the forest, the large amount of wilderness designations, where development is prohibited, creates an isolated region of mountains and rugged canyons with few roads or structures.

For Tour Divide riders, this remote area covers the longest food re-supply stretch of the route. The only "service" for 200 miles is the Beaverhead Work Center, run by the U.S. Forest Service, that offers potable water and a soda machine.

In addition to the remoteness, the onslaught of the summer monsoon season that begins in early July (exactly the time I rode through) poses another challenge. The storms bring rain that combine with the natural clay surface to create impassable roads, and the lightning that accompanies it routinely sparks forest fires.

Before reaching the work center, I had to cross the Continental Divide three times. Each crossing consisted of a small climb followed by a short downhill. No big deal under clear conditions. However, the clouds were now almost on top of us. We could see that rain was already falling on the roads a few miles in front of us.

After the first crossing, several motorcycles rode past us around the Collins Park area, making a right turn to exit the Gila before the rain caught them. Nic and I didn't have that option, and we pressed forward. We made a left turn to ride the final two divide crossings before Beaverhead. Sprinkles of rain and mist fell on us as we climbed the tree lined road.

Cresting the third and final divide crossing, we reached mile marker 81.2 on the map. The notation at that mile marker states "Ranch on right. Ride into open grasslands and dramatically different surroundings. Fencing next two miles." Oh, how right they were about that one. The views opened up revealing grasslands and very few trees.

The good news was the pounding rain had already hit this section, and the clouds were moving away from us. The bad news was that the dirt road had been turned into a two-mile mud pit. This was the beginning of the Gila mud fight. I would have preferred riding in the rain rather than through the mud. Especially the Gila mud that clings to everything and causes the bike to become almost unrideable.

We had no option but to keep riding. The road was slightly downhill so my technique was to maintain as much speed as possible before I hit each mud pit, hoping the bike would go mostly straight and bring me out the other end. On many occasions, the bike slid way off to one side causing me to put a foot down in the sloppy mud. Twice, my bike slid violently enough to throw me off, sending me rolling through the mud. I laughed at the situation, and provided plenty of comedy for Nic who laughed as he watched me pick myself up out of the mud.

Eventually, the mud torpedoed Nic, sending him face first into the slop. Finally, I got to laugh at one of his wipeouts instead of laughing at my own. It felt good to ride with a friend. We both laughed at the comical situation, rather than getting too frustrated with the conditions.

That is until we passed those two miles of fencing mentioned in the map. When we got to the open area, the mud had dried out enough to turn from slop into stick-to-everything mud. It would have made some great adobe or pottery. It did not make a good road surface. Each revolution of my tires picked up pounds of mud that adhered to the tires and the bike frame. Within fifty feet, the bike would no longer roll because it was so heavily clogged with mud. Using my fingers to pull clobs of mud from between the frame and back tire, I could get the bike to roll another fifty feet. Pull off more mud. Roll another fifty feet. Repeat. It was a no win situation. We were literally stuck in the mud in the middle of the afternoon.

"This isn't going to work! It will take hours to go a mile with this mud," I said to Nic.

"Yeah, we can't get through this," he replied.

"Too bad we missed the rain. It would have been rideable during the downpour," I said while still pulling clumps of mud from my bike.

"We could wait for it to dry out," Nic said.

"We could setup camp and get a nap while it dries. But I hate to stop this early."

"I know. Hey, the cows are moving through the deep grass. Maybe it's not quite as sticky over there."

"It's worth a shot. Better than staying here." I said.

Pushing (ok, mostly carrying our bikes still caked with mud) through a half mile of muddy grass took us well over an hour. It was grueling, slow going. Even the cows looked at us like we were crazy to be navigating through the mud. I kept thinking of The Clash's "I Fought the Law" song, but in my head I sang, *I fought the Gila and the Gila won.*

Eventually, the road surface became more gravelly and rideable. The day faded into night, with the rain clouds returning to intermittently sprinkle us as we pushed on towards the Beaverhead Work Center. Instead of fighting through the mud, we now navigated around hundreds of tiny frogs covering the road. Occasionally, we heard the unfortunate "squish" of a frog meeting our bike tires.

At the Work Center, I refilled my water and took a short break. When I saw the vending machine, I got excited about having a Coke to keep me going. That is until Nic informed me it was out of service, crushing my dreams of more sugar and caffeine. As we sat at the Work Center, a steady rain started to fall again.

All of the mud and grit had worn down the brake pads; they could slow my bike, but not really stop it. The first downhill after the Work Center was fast with some tight turns. Combine that with rain and darkness and you have one sketchy descent. Nic once again showed his great handling skills and descended much, much faster than me. Once safely at the bottom, we stopped to adjust our brake pads to give us better stopping power.

The forty-seven miles from the Beaverhead Work Center to the exit of the Gila were filled with constant climbs and descents. I managed to make it over one more climb before I realized that I would not be making it out of the Gila that night. My ankles simply would not let me keep going; it was after midnight on a day that I had covered over 140 miles in nineteen hours. I was worn out, wet, and sleepy.

Nic was ahead of me and I couldn't stop without letting him know my plan. I needed to let him know he didn't have to wait for me. I struggled to keep going, and eventually his headlight came into view in the distance as he took a short break.

"Hey man, I can't go any further. I have to stop," I said as I caught up to him.

"Are you sure? We can make it to the pavement at least," Nic replied.

"No, I'm done. With my ankles like they are, I have to stop for the night."

"I'm running low on food and want to get closer to Silver City. I'm going to keep riding," Nic said.

"Ok, good luck." I watched him remount his bike and ride off in the mud and rain.

Stopping at that point left me almost 200 miles from the finish in Antelope Wells. Would I be able to catch up to him the following day? Was he pushing through the night and going for the finish? How could he keep riding through the mud and the rain after we had already put in so many miles through mud that day? My gut feeling told me that I would not see him on the road to the finish. With his riding abilities and his drive to push himself further, he was destined to finish hours ahead of me.

I pitched my tarp and cozied up in my down quilt just as the rain started to fall again with much more force. I was happy to be comfortable and dry, especially considering that my first thought upon stopping was to simply lay down under a tree without taking the time and energy to set up my tarp.

Eventually, my body drifted off to a few hours of fitful sleep. I hoped this sleep would recharge me enough to pedal out of the of the cruel Gila Wilderness and finish my adventure.

36

Adventure Books

THOUGHTS OF ADVENTURE HAD BEEN in my mind since I was a kid in South Carolina building tree forts and playing in the woods behind my house. Out in the woods I usually found myself in the midst of a survival game, or fending off the "bad guys" in an epic battle as I hunkered down in my tree fort. Even though I was only a few hundred feet from my house, in my mind I was hundreds or even thousands of miles away.

Playing in the woods was more fun for me than reading. The only type of books I read were adventure books. *My Side of the Mountain* by Jean Craighead George is the one I remember most. In the book, Sam Gribley (who must have been around thirteen years old), runs away from his New York home and heads alone into the Catskills to live in the mountains. He struggles at first, but learns to live off of the land, make a house inside the trunk of a giant tree, and survive the harsh winter. It was a story that any kid who loved the outdoors could enjoy.

After reading *My Side of the Mountain* there were plenty of days where I was Sam Gribley foraging for food, making improvements to my shelter, and living on my own. While my family had three TV channels and an Atari console for inside entertainment, I loved to go outside and make up my own adventures.

While preparing for the Tour Divide, I re-read *My Side of the Mountain* and enjoyed it as much as when I was younger. Towards the end of the book, Sam Gribley meets a boy from town, and the boy asks Sam why he is in the woods:

> "Well, the falcon takes the sky, the white-throated sparrow takes the low bushes, the skunk takes the earth, you take the newspaper office. I take the woods."

As a kid, Sam's adventure was a fantastic, if unrealistic, dream. Books like *The Call of the Wild* by Jack London and *Tracks Across Alaska* by Alastair Scott also fueled my thoughts of adventure. I could picture myself in the cold snow, traveling across Alaska with my sled dogs leading the way.

What is at about the adventure stories that grabbed my attention? It wasn't like I wanted to take sled dogs into the Yukon or on the Iditarod trail (although both of those do sound like fun). I wasn't really going to live out in the woods by myself, leaving behind my mom's homemade bread or my grandma's fried chicken and white gravy.

It was simply the pull of being "out there" similar to what Buck experienced in *The Call of the Wild*:

> "It filled him with a great unrest and strange desires. It caused him to feel a vague, sweet gladness, and he was aware of wild yearning and stirrings for he knew not what."

The stories feature ordinary people overcoming struggles, resulting in extraordinary adventures. The stories of world class athletes training and winning championships didn't attract me;

those "best of the best" type athletes were too distant from what I was or could be. However, I could relate to a boy going out in the woods, or a man being out of his element and tackling the Iditarod trail for the first time.

The struggle and triumph of the common man brought me to these books. I'm a sucker for the Rocky, Rudy, David and Goliath, "little guy works his butt off to make it" stories. The struggle, possibility of failure, and difficulties along the way bring out the real story, allowing us to experience the success or failure of the characters involved.

Throughout the books, characters struggled, pushing themselves to the limit to survive and reach their goals. Why would they continue to endure the pain and exhaustion? Why not just give up and call it a day?

I look to my buddy Sam Gribley for the answer, as he describes welcoming the beginning of another day in the woods:

"Fortunately, the sun has a wonderfully glorious habit of rising every morning. When the sky lightened, when the birds awoke, I knew I would never again see anything as splendid as the round red sun coming up over the earth."

The brief moments where we can see the beauty of the world make the struggle to get there worth it. Those few minutes where mind, body, and soul are perfectly aligned, and it feels like no effort is needed to make progress. Many have called it flow, or zen, or bliss. When it occurs, it is so special. Just like when the weather finally broke as I climbed Huckleberry Pass outside of Ovando, allowing me to pedal up the mountain and leave behind the snow and cold and doubt as if the mountain were nothing more than a small hill. These moments are the reason so much effort, heartache, and suffering can be tolerated.

The Gila Wilderness still held me in its grip, not letting me go without more suffering. Thirty years after imagining myself in my childhood adventure books, there I was in the depths of my own quest, experiencing all of the highs and lows that go along with those stories. My dream of adventure was no longer a dream. I made it a reality.

Now I needed to write the final chapter of my Tour Divide story.

37

The Finish

WOULD THIS BE THE FINAL sunrise for me on this adventure? Was 190 miles in one day possible?

It was time to find out.

As I began my day at 6:00 a.m., the morning was filled with a light mist and a low cloud cover. I expected to ride the final 190 miles solo. Nic had continued on through the night, and I figured he was miles and miles ahead of me by now. I ate a Milky Way and instant coffee (a strange but surprisingly delicious combination), and began my struggle to leave the Gila. I realized Nita's kindness and generosity was still with me. Without my meal at the Toaster House, I would have been out of food and forced to ride into Silver City with only crumbs left in my bike bags.

I felt good on the first of two climbs to exit the Gila. The second one, not so much. The overnight rain turned the road into sticky mud that clogged my drivetrain. I pushed my bike up the road, frustrated with the conditions. I thought about Nic and what he must have encountered riding through the area during the early morning hours in the pouring rain.

After two hours of slogging in the mud, I made it to the top of the final climb. Only a downhill remained until I reached pavement. But this was the Gila, and it wasn't going to let me out of its grip easily. Instead of smooth sailing, the downhill contained the worst kind of washboard known to mankind! At times, the entire width of the road was one giant washboard. There was no alternative but to bounce and rattle and shake through it. I rode into these sections with as much speed as possible, while my hands, teeth, and bike all chattered over the washboards. Once the washboard slowed me to a crawl, I bounced and pedaled through the remaining section. This happened over and over again.

I remember yelling out at the road several times after I had been thrown around so badly that my chain fell off. Luckily, no gear bounced out or broke off. Finally, I made it to the pavement section. I was done with the Gila and it had definitely won. It had practically broken me.

On the road, I passed a number of washouts where sand, rocks, and mud covered the road. The previous night's storm must have delivered a lot more rain that I thought. Still reeling from the defeat of the Gila, I let the Gila get one more sucker punch in the fight. In a moment of defeat, I decided to ride the paved alternate rather than taking the seven miles of CDT singletrack that are part of the official Tour Divide route.

The paved alternate was an official option this year due to some confusing signage stating the CDT sections was closed. I knew it was open and I could have taken it, but I didn't want to see any more of that Gila-type mud. Seeing the washouts along the road, I figured that section would be a mud slog like Nic and

I had experienced the night before, full of walking and cleaning mud off of the bike simply to make it roll another ten feet.

How does someone that loves riding singletrack pass up one of the few singletrack sections in the entire race? Looking back now, I really wish I had taken the CDT section. The Gila had beaten and battered my body and mind.

The road route turned out to be really steep - not an easy path at all. It was a beautiful area to ride and walk through. Yep, once again I did a lot of walking on a paved road.

All of the frustration from the Gila, the washboards, and the steep climbs faded away on the downhill into Silver City. Being tucked into the aero bars swooping through turns has a way of easing my mind.

A welcomed surprise awaited me in Silver City. Nic was still there, and I met up with him at a breakfast café.

"Hey man, I didn't expect to see you here! I thought you would be close to the finish by now. How far did you ride last night?" I asked.

"I made it through the CDT alternate section and had to stop at one of the campgrounds around 4:00," Nic replied.

"Wow, I don't know how you kept riding that late and with the constant rain. There is no way I would have made it that far."

"It was hard. I dozed off a couple of times while riding, but I got a few hours of sleep at the campground. I've been here in Silver City for a couple of hours."

The restaurant allowed me to order a big plate of biscuits and gravy, eggs, sausage, and hash browns before they closed. It was going to be great to share the finish with Nic. Not only was he a friend that started the race with me, but he had built my bike piece by piece, and offered so many tips during our training rides and chats in the bike shop. I owed a lot of my Tour Divide success to him.

Before leaving town, we stopped at a gas station for our final re-supply.

"Hey Nic, have you ever started a century ride in the middle of the afternoon?" I asked as we climbed on a paved road leaving Silver City.

"Nope," he replied.

"Well, now we can say we have. Let's knock out this century."

We still had 120 miles to cover to make the finish. It was going to be a long, long night.

Of course, as we turned onto the final miles of dirt for the Tour Divide, we got caught in another thunderstorm. It wouldn't be the 2014 Tour Divide if there wasn't bad weather on the final day. We started with days of rain and snow. It felt appropriate to finish with several days of rain and mud.

We took cover under a small tree, and waited for the worst of the storm to pass over. Once back on the bikes, it was muddy but easy riding. As the cool air from the storm turned back to desert heat, Nic managed to take off his rain jacket and rain pants as he rode. Not sure how he accomplished that feat; the man has some serious bike skills.

A nice surprise awaited us at the Separ exit where the route crossed under interstate I-10. What looked like a souvenir store actually had snacks, drinks, and frozen burritos in the back. Score! We sat outside on the porch as we ate, watching the sun drop lower and lower on the horizon. We were now so close, we knew we would finish that night. The question was what time.

The last seventy miles would be in darkness with only our headlights to guide us to the finish.

On the twenty-five-mile stretch from Separ to Hachita, the tiredness took over and I began to fall asleep on the bike. Every mile became a struggle. It's not easy to stay awake when you're riding in complete darkness on a flat paved road after covering more than 140 miles for the day. At 11:00 p.m., we rolled into Hachita, both of us dragging and wondering how we would finish the final forty-five miles.

We stopped for a snack break, and neither of us was looking forward to getting back on the bike. I looked at Nic, saw the same blankness in his eyes and asked "Quick nap?"

"Yeah, that might be good," he agreed.

We set alarms on our phones and laid down on the picnic tables to grab fifteen minutes of sleep. Closing my eyes and drifting off for a light nap was just what I needed. Leaving Hachita, Nic was even more rested. He quickly pedaled away from me; his light disappearing in the distance. It was just me and the darkness of the desert. A fitting finish to the Tour Divide.

After riding a few miles, my iPod came out of my front storage pocket for the fourth time in the entire race. There I was with my music, my bike, and the desert laid out before me. The scene reminds me of those few words I always saw my dad type out when he sat down at a typewriter - "Now is the time for all good men..." This was my time. The finish was within reach, just a mere three hours away. Ok, not really a "mere" three hours. More like a long trance-like three hours.

The music helped me get into a nice groove. After 2700 miles of racing, I discovered my legs still had a bit left in them. I was going to finish, but I had one last mind game to play. A finish time before 3:00 a.m. was my new goal if for no other reason than pride. Why finish at 3:14 a.m. when I could finish at 2:59 a.m. Instead? I didn't want that last hour to tick over before I reached Antelope Wells. Every tenth of a mile was marked on the road so I could see exactly how much progress I made. The game consisted of staying in the aero bars for three or four tenths of a mile, standing up and cranking for a tenth of a mile, and earning a snack once I passed specific mile markers.

As I was cranking away I caught a glimpse of Nic's bike leaning against a post at the side of the road. He had stopped for another little snooze. I stopped too, to wake him up and get him moving again. I felt a little bad about waking him up, but I knew that if either of us laid down for more than a few minutes, we would have been out for hours. We could sleep after the finish. At that moment, we had pedaling to do.

Soon after, we saw car lights and people waving their arms, which caused me to think it was some sort of border guard or someone getting me to stop and talk to them. Funny what your brain thinks at 1:00 a.m. on a border road. Instead we were greeted with cheers and cowbells from Nic's family, who had driven back up from the border to give us a little encouragement.

Nic and I rode side-by-side in the final stretch, completely focused on our own ride with our own music and pedals cranking. This was one of my favorite parts of the ride even though there was no laughing, no views, and no mountains to see. The world contracted, reduced to a pair of cyclists giving it everything they had to complete their dream ride.

Neither of us glanced over. We focused on the road ahead, and kept the pace high. During this stretch, we never got more than about twenty yards ahead or behind the other. While we were physically so close on the road, mentally we were each in our own bubble, not willing to slow down or let the sleep monster creep up on us.

At 2:00 a.m., tired and worn out, I caught the finest second wind of my riding career. I felt so alive. Nothing could stop me. My legs pedaled strong, pushing me closer and closer to the border at more than 17 mph. Ten miles were all that remained in my 2745 mile journey. I knew I would finish the Tour Divide within an hour. But would I make it there by my arbitrary 3:00 a.m. goal?

Before the finish, Nic and I wanted to do a little bit of racing. I thought we'd race the final 200 yards once we saw the border. Nic? He had other plans. He looked at me with three miles to go and yelled, "Let's race!!"

That race (if you want to call it that) lasted all of three pedal strokes. Nic, being a much stronger rider than me, darted off in front of me as I tried to catch up. Which soon turned into struggling to keep a constant gap between us. Before long, I merely tried to keep his light in view.

In those final two miles, the emotions finally hit me. I was actually going to finish this race. After all of the years of preparation and planning, my dream was becoming a reality. I would say it was becoming a reality in front of my eyes, except it was almost 3:00 a.m. and I couldn't see beyond the beam of my headlight. On that final day, I managed to cover 190 miles even with a swollen ankle that had severely limited my miles since crossing the Colorado border all those days ago. You never know what you are capable of until you try.

The last song that came on my iPod was "Lose Yourself" by Eminem. It's a song I had used for motivation in my training. It's funny how sometimes a shuffled playlist chooses the perfect song for the moment. I was taking my one shot. I was definitely seizing my opportunity.

My race ended at 2:58 a.m. with a finish time of 23 days, 18 hours, and 58 minutes. I had done it! Little ole me rode his bike from Canada to Mexico.

Nic had arrived a minute before me. I rolled up next to him, gave him a giant hug, and let the feeling of being finished wash over me.

I was a Tour Divide finisher. It took everything I had, and forced me to rethink what was possible. Dreams do come true.

38

Epilogue

I N WRITING THIS BOOK, I'VE had the opportunity to look back on my ride, the ups and downs, and the decisions I could have made differently. And I realize I would not change a thing, except maybe taking that last singletrack option.

Had I ridden more on some days or done things different, I wouldn't have had my Gilligan's Island ride with Nic, ridden over Fleecer Ridge around midnight with Alice, seen a mountain lion, or shared a tipi with Scotty.

Those are the items I remember about the race, not the exact mileages, efficient (or lack thereof) re-supply stops, or my final placing.

What started as a race became more about the adventure and the people, not my finish time or overall placing.

What am I doing now?

As I write this, it's been two years since I embarked on the 2014 Tour Divide. The time has included a lot more time with my family, a few sporadic bike rides, and absolutely no training of any kind. If the weather is not favorable, I don't have to ride.

Recovering from the Tour Divide experience took me six months. I didn't do any, biking, running, or moving for the first month after I returned home, letting my body rest and heal. The numbness in my hands and soreness in my ankles eventually faded.

I enjoy bike riding as much as ever, but in much smaller quantities. Bikepacking trips now include a casual agenda complete with a stove, coffee in the morning, time around a campfire, and enjoying the adventure. My kids enjoy an occasional bikepacking or backpacking trip with dad. Those are the trips I'm most excited about.

Life. Family. Not as much riding.

THE END

One of Andy's rare dry moments on the first day.

Another rider struggles up the infamous Connector Trail in the Flathead Valley.

A warm welcome on the way into Helena, Montana

Being chased by a thunderstorm outside of Lima, Montana

Wide open views of the Wind River Range outside Pinedale, Wyoming

Sunrise in the Great Basin

Andy is happy after a giant breakfast and coffee at Brush Mountain Lodge.

Tipi in Sargents, Colorado. Photo by Ken Scott.

Nic Handy enjoys pie in Pie Town!

Nita and Andy at the Toaster House in Pie Town, New Mexico. Photo by Nic Handy.

Forgotten church along the backroads of New Mexico.

3:00 a.m. at the finish! Tired, muddy, and happy. Photo by Nic Handy.

Appendix

Gear List

Bike Components

Moots Mooto X YBB 29er
J. Paks H-BarPak handlebar bag
J. Paks SeatPak
J. Paks custom frame bag
J. Paks SnakPak gas tank bag
Jones H Bar
Schmidt SON Delux dynamo front hub
Busch & Müller Luxos U dynamo light with USB port
Rohloff Speedhub 14 speed internally gear rear hub
Vision aero bars

Clothing (Total Weight 45.41 oz)

Buff headwear (1.38 oz)
Smartwool arm warmers (1.90 oz)
Pearl Izumi leg warmers (3.88 oz)
Manzella lobster gloves (3.00 oz)
ZPacks rain mitts (0.86 oz)
Homemade cuben fiber booties (0.67 oz)

Smartwool socks (2.00 oz)

GoLite Virga rain jacket (7.84 oz)

Campmor rain pants (7.25 oz)

GoLite wool undershirt (4.68 oz)

Minus33 wool boxers (3.00 oz)

Pearl Izumi toe warmers (3.00 oz)

Montbell short sleeve down jacket (5.95 oz)

Sleep System (Total Weight 53.58 oz)

ZPacks Hexamid tarp (5.29 oz)

Carbon fiber tarp pole (1.45 oz)

GoLite 30 degree down quilt (21.29 oz)

Borah bivy (6.00 oz)

Big Agnes Q Core SL sleeping pad (16.58 oz)

KookaBay pillow and cover (2.97 oz)

First Aid / Repair / Personal Care (Total Weight 52.99 oz)

Gear repair kit (5.14 oz)

Bike repair kit (5.36 oz)

2 spare tubes (12.64 oz)

Lezyne pump (3.17 oz)

Spare spokes (0.48 oz)

Chain lube (0.65 oz)

Pale Spruce StayOutThere kit (9.78 oz)

Bear spray (11.26 oz)

Wallet and passport (2.79 oz)

Mini bike lock (1.72 oz)

Electronics / Navigation (Total Weight 28.05 oz)

iPhone 5 with case and charger (9.38 oz)
iPod Shuffle and charger (1.57 oz)
SPOT tracker (4.18 oz)
Garmin eTrex 20 GPS (5.00 oz)
Adventure Cycling map set (7.92 oz)

Food / Water (Total Weight 14.49 oz)

1L Platypus soft bottle (0.89 oz)
Sawyer mini filter (2.00 oz)
100oz Camelbak bladder (7.20 oz)
Emergency food (3.00 oz)
Foldable backpack (1.40 oz)

ABOUT THE AUTHOR

Growing up in South Carolina, Andy Amick dreamed of adventures while building forts and playing in the woods. Once he discovered the joy of mountain biking during high school, he became instantly hooked. The lure of pedaling through the mountains brought him to Boulder, Colorado, where adventures awaited at every turn.

He never looked back. The next twenty years found him enjoying a variety of outdoor activities. He and his wife continue to call Colorado home. When not working as a Software Engineer, he shares his love of the mountains with his two sons.

Printed in Great Britain
by Amazon

34337378R10158